Light Japan

Memories of Japan and Cambridge as members of OMF 1995-2022

ROGER & JEA-NAM STEVENS

LOXWOOD PRESS

Copyright © Roger & Jea-Nam Stevens

All rights reserved
No part of this publication may be reproduced
or transmitted in any form or by any means, electronic
or mechanical, including photocopy, recording or any
information storage and retrieval system, without permission
in writing from the publisher or the author.

ISBN 978-1-908113-74-0

Published 2024 by Loxwood Press,
50 Loxwood Avenue, Worthing,
West Sussex BN14 7RA.
Tel: 01903 232208

Designed and printed by Atelier82 Ltd,
24-25 South Road, Harlow, Essex CM20 2AR.
Tel: 01279 212923
hello@atelier82.co.uk

LIGHTS TO JAPAN
Memories of our years with OMF

わたしがあなたがたを休ませてあげます。

Jesus said, "I will give you rest"
(Matthew 11:28)

OMF INTERNATIONAL

OMF International is an international and interdenominational Evangelical Christian missionary society with an international centre in Singapore.
It was founded in Britain by Hudson Taylor on 25 June 1865 and was called China Inland Mission (CIM).

Contents

Introduction

1	How it all started	7
2	Life at University	9
3	J Nam's story	16
4	Japan, not Africa	19
5	Further hurdles to overcome	23
6	OMF missionaries in Japan – at last!	27
7	Snow and slush	30
8	Leading a Japanese church	34
9	Home Assignment	47
10	Back to Japan	49
11	Second Home Assignment	58
12	Opportunities and problems	61

PART TW0
2009 – 2022

Ministry to Japanese in Cambridge   79

Introduction

THIS book was originally intended primarily – though by no means only – as a 'thank you' to those who prayed for us and supported us during the years we served as members of OMF International, firstly in Japan and then in Cambridge. However, the publishers felt it would be of interest to a wider readership and so it has been expanded somewhat. It's very largely from Roger's memory (but also J Nam and for a few things, our daughter Angela) so some details may not be completely accurate! However, it's funny how memories come back as one thinks and writes, talks, reminisces – though occasionally there have been disagreements!

Some memories are embarrassing, but mostly they are encouraging as we recall what the Lord, by His grace, has done for and in us. The greatest memory is how God has reconciled us to Himself through the death and resurrection of Jesus. However, without boasting, we can also recall what the Lord has done through us as we have aspired to love and serve Him, despite many weaknesses and failings. Whoever we are and wherever we may be, we can expect God to work through us by His Spirit to contribute towards the building of His kingdom. So, God's work for and in us and God's work *through* us is all because of His grace.

J Nam and I pray that as you read this small book God will use it in your life to bless you; we hope that you will find something that is interesting, informative and inspiring.

Roger and J Nam Stevens

1
How it all started

WHEN does our story start? Was it when we were welcomed as members of OMF in January 1994 at the end of a Candidates Course in the UK? Or was it more than a year later when we arrived in Japan? Or was it several weeks before that when we received our first OMF allowance – in Singaporean dollar banknotes – just after arriving in Singapore for the Orientation Course? I remember feeling that then we were really members of OMF! The story begins earlier however.

I was born on May 21st 1956 and brought up in Southampton. The UK was coming out of post-war austerity and rationing had finally ended that year. I was unaware of any shortages or lack of anything. Until I was about 14, we lived without a telephone, a fridge or a car, but I thought nothing of it. However, many years later Mum told me she often had to watch the pennies, especially at the end of the annual week's family holiday by the sea.

My father worked at Dock House at Southampton Docks, though I never really understood what he did there except that he worked in an office. We lived in a council house and I think he was the only man to go off to work wearing a suit and hat. My mother was a full-time housewife, which was the norm then, though she took on some part-time clerical work when I was in my early teens. My childhood memories of home-life are very happy ones. My parents brought me and my brother and sister up lovingly.

School-life I would describe as okay, even quite enjoyable at times. However, I preferred the holidays! Apart from the first day or two, just before my fifth birthday, I did the ten-to-15-minute walk to school and back on my own. There was no "school run" then! The interests I developed were mainly outside school life, toy cars and model animals, miniature plastic soldiers and Airfix models of tanks, warplanes and warships – which Dad was usually persuaded to do the work of assembling! There were favourite television programmes and discovering books – mostly factual on subjects like dinosaurs, although I became a Sherlock Holmes fan. I was fascinated when a teacher read to us *"The Lion, the Witch and the Wardrobe"*, though I didn't know any of the Christian parallels. There was playing and watching football, especially after the 1966 World Cup. A table football game, subbuteo occupied me for years. Later I got a part-time job selling programmes at the Southampton football ground. During my mid-teens I became interested in chess and at Sixth Form College became a fanatic, playing for the school and then the college team, studying the game every day after finishing school homework.

When I was about ten years old a weekly comic I enjoyed reading was *"The Victor"*. One of the serialised stories was "Stark of the Samurai", about an English Samurai in feudal Japan and this inspired me at school to write a story in which I was in Japan in the city of Nagoya. I found this place on a map and used it as it seemed more interesting than well-known places like Tokyo and Osaka.

It was my father who – no doubt unintentionally – aroused my curiosity about the Japanese. He had been based in Singapore as a soldier during World War II and was there when the Japanese attacked. Fortunately, he was one of those who managed to get away just before Singapore was taken, but this experience and later hearing of war-time atrocities done by the Japanese armies impacted my dad very negatively, as was the case for many of his generation. Though he was generally a quiet, gentle man, I sensed a definite hostility to the Japanese people when I asked him about the war. That surprised me because he didn't show the same feelings towards the Germans. The memory stayed with me.

In 1975 I gained admission to the University of Birmingham to read my favourite subject, History, and in my first year I took a hugely significant step which was to change radically the direction of my life.

2
Life at University

Nearly an atheist

I WAS excited to go to university, but life did not turn out as I'd expected. The novelty of living away from home soon faded and one of the goals I had set myself proved to be out of reach. One I had already failed. I had applied for Cambridge University but had not been accepted; a great blow to my academic ambitions. The other two goals remained; to excel at chess (perhaps become champion of Britain!) and to find a girlfriend. Very soon the first goal was dashed when I discovered I wasn't good enough for the university's 1st team and the second wasn't realised mainly, I think, because of my shyness. So, I became rather disillusioned with life.

It was at this time that, for the first time in my life, I saw someone change because of putting their faith in Christ. I was waiting in line for lunch in a university canteen and commented to a fellow history student, "We have that boring religious history lecture this afternoon." Imagine my astonishment at her reply, "Wash your mouth out with soap!" It transpired that Sue had recently become 'religious'. We had a vigorous discussion about her new beliefs; I could see the change was very real for her, but I just felt she'd been brain-washed and said to myself, "I'll never believe all that."

I'd not been brought up to go to church and was close to being an atheist, having hardly ever thought about God or religion. Yet, a spark of curiosity had been ignited and I accepted a Christian book, *"Live a New Life"* by David Watson, from her. In it I was struck by the words of Jesus, *"Come to me all who labour and are heavy laden and I will give you rest."* I must admit that I was attracted to Sue and so when she invited me to church that factor overcame my wariness of what I might be getting into! As I had never been to church, except for weddings, a funeral and school carol services, I wondered what happened on an ordinary Sunday. I told myself it'd probably just be a gathering of a small number of elderly ladies.

In fact, church turned out to be another big surprise with around 400 in the congregation, many students and young people. I was impressed by the atmosphere in the service and by the sincerity of the preacher and I went away thinking, "I don't know if I believe what he said but he certainly does!"

I became more serious in my seeking and as I read the one Christian book I had I began to feel as if here was what I'd been looking for all my life, but I'd never considered 'religion' or the Bible. I prayed a simple prayer, "Oh God, if You are really there, show me." And He did, in an unusual way.

At this time, with questions about God and the meaning of life absorbing my attention, my chess hobby had suddenly become unimportant and my desire to play had disappeared. I was due to play in a match for the university and only reluctantly turned up so that I wouldn't let the others down. Then to my surprise I found myself playing without any tension, as had normally been the case when I was striving to win. It seemed as if I were being guided by God in my moves and I won the game easily. I now felt sure about God's reality, that He had revealed Himself to me. I joined the team for the usual drink in the students' bar but I was itching to get back to my digs in order to pray the prayer of commitment at the back of, *"Live a New Life"*. So it was that on March 18 1976, alone in my room, I asked God to forgive my sins and I put my faith in Jesus Christ. It was the last day of term.

The next morning, I was absolutely full of joy, on cloud nine. I travelled home by train for the Easter holiday and read John's gospel (it was a little booklet; I don't remember how I'd got hold of it) but it so gripped me that I read it right through to the end without stopping.

Greatest event
This encounter with Christ was the greatest event in my life, gave me inner peace and a purpose for living and was eventually to result in my becoming a mission worker in Japan.

I told my 15-year-old sister what had happened to me. She was the only one in our family who had any spiritual interest. She went to church and had been led to Christ by her Sunday school teacher when she was about ten years old. She was really pleased to hear about my conversion and told me she'd been praying for me! Later she helped me find a local church where I met a lively group of young people – one of them remains one of my best friends. I was baptised in September 1977 and was encouraged that my parents came to witness the event.

Soon after my conversion I became involved with a student Christian group, the Navigators, who helped me to get into the Bible and grow spiritually to know Christ better. Christian books were very helpful. One habit I acquired early on was having a daily time (or devotions) with God. I remember joining a weekend-away at which several of us shared a room. Upon waking up the first morning I was surprised to find that they were all reading their Bibles! Since then, for 48 years, I have greatly profited from having a morning quiet time; though there have been occasions when I've missed having it.

Christian growth wasn't always smooth and I have faced my share of temptations and failure. One thing I struggled with was a poor self-image which gave me an inferiority complex (or occasionally, superiority!) and change in this area has been slow.

I regularly attended a large, quite charismatic Anglican church that I had first visited before believing. There was good, Bible-based teaching and the uplifting Sunday worship contributed to giving me a thirst to experience God more. Books I came across by A.W. Tozer, which I found very insightful and inspiring, also stimulated this desire. At the end of a special service one evening in autumn 1978 I had a fresh, powerful encounter with God. Repentance in floods of tears was followed by great joy and a boldness to share Jesus with others. Somewhat strangely though, a few weeks later I entered a dark period during which there were moments I doubted everything about the Christian faith. I had the opportunity to share this experience and it was pointed out to me that immediately after Jesus was baptised and the Holy Spirit descended on Him, Jesus was led into the wilderness to be tempted by the devil. I gradually came back into a more 'normal' walk with God.

Part of the discipleship teaching of the Navigators was on world vision. I already had an interest in the world, mainly through my love of history and maps, and so it wasn't long before I began to develop an interest in what God was doing worldwide. This was partly through reading the biography of Hudson Taylor, which impressed and inspired me. I also became much more aware of the international students around me. Doing a year of teacher training after I'd graduated, I met Sumi, a Japanese student. I knew nothing about Christianity in Japan and as we ate together in the hall's dining room, I directly asked him if he was a Christian. His unexpected answer was, "Not yet." It transpired that he'd been impressed by a Christian university lecturer in Japan. Clearly some seed-sowing had already been done, quite unusual for Japanese because Christians are so few, as I would find out years later.

Our friendship developed and during the Easter vacation I invited him to stay a night or two at my parents' home. This appeared to have a good impact on my father as it was his first personal contact with someone from Japan. For a while I saw less of my Japanese friend and then one day when we met up, he told me he'd come to faith in Christ!

In 1981 as his time to return to Japan was drawing near, he invited me to visit him. Going to the other side of the world had never entered my mind and seemed impossible, but the idea was exciting. I'd never flown before and I knew it would be expensive, but amazingly God opened up a way for me to go to Japan that summer. My brother had just obtained a job with British Airways and this meant I could get a cheap flight to Japan. He came with me and for three weeks we had a great time travelling around in some of the big cities and also staying with some of my friend's relatives.

When I returned to the UK, I had a burning desire to go back to Japan and started praying that God would open up the way for me. Through international contacts within the Navigators, I met one of their Japanese staff, Ichimura-san ('san' means Mr, Mrs or Miss), who was visiting London. He invited me to assist in his ministry in Tokyo and I went out at the end of August 1982. A few months before going I had further evidence that the Lord was indeed leading me this way. The Navigator group I was part of had a workshop on discovering one's gifts and mine came out as preaching (surprisingly as I'd had almost no experience!), teaching and evangelism. The next day at church someone who knew I was interested in Japan gave me a magazine because it had an article about mission in Japan. The article said that Japan needed workers who were gifted in ... preaching, teaching and evangelism.

I spent just over two and a half memorable years in Tokyo, teaching English part-time and participating in the ministry of the Navigators. I also studied Japanese and was encouraged by the progress I made. I particularly appreciated Ichimura-san, who mentored and cared for me. I also got to know well Ogo-san, my Japanese flat-mate. There were times when things were difficult, mainly in the first year after the initial excitement and novelty had worn off. I had feelings of loneliness, especially at Christmas, and was frustrated with making so little progress in the Japanese language. On one occasion I was in a Christian meeting and after a few minutes, having given up trying to understand the Japanese, I started reading my Bible. Very soon the words, "I will bring you back to this land." (Genesis 28:15) leaped out of the page and struck me powerfully. My immediate reaction was 'Oh no! Surely not'. It was difficult to ignore what I'd read but when it was time to return home, my attitude had completely changed and I was sorry to leave Japan!

Back in the UK I felt strongly that Japan would feature significantly in my future, though I was unsure how that would work out. Furthermore, how much was its God's leading and how much was it what I wanted? As one of the few westerners in Japan it was quite appealing to often be the centre of attention, especially with Japanese girls. (One lady said I looked like the film star, Omar Sharif!) However, God gave me more guidance. I found out that Matthew 11:28, the verse that had been the most instrumental in my conversion, was the same verse that featured most in Japanese coming to Christ. *"Come to me, all who labour and are heavy laden, and I will give you rest."* Another issue I struggled with was whether I should return as an English teacher or as a missionary. * The words in Matthew 28:17, *"but some doubted"*, immediately before Jesus gave the Great Commission, showed me that 'full-time' workers are by no means perfect. I'd had an inflated image of what kind of a person a missionary was, but came to see that whether a missionary or an English teacher (or whatever) is not a matter of what is better but of God's calling.

However, for a couple of years or so things did not go as I planned. I studied at London Bible College (LBC), but shortage of finances meant spreading a one-year course over two years. For a few weeks I had time to do some personal research that related to my sense of a call to Japan. I wanted to learn about Shinto, Buddhism, Confucianism and Japanese 'new religions' and, accessing the college library, I made use of every relevant book (not that many!) I could find.

Before long, however, I needed to find part-time work. My main job was as a school cleaner, which I was initially very reluctant to take, mainly because of my pride ("surely with my qualifications and experience I can find something better!"). I needed the money and eventually took the job. And God taught me a valuable lesson in that I learned to do the job as, "working for the Lord and not for people" (Colossians 3:23) and even found joy in doing it. Later I even recruited two or three other LBC students who needed some holiday work.

*The word "missionary" is difficult to define accurately and nowadays is used in different ways. I am using the word as it was traditionally understood then as someone whose work is with a church or Christian organisation abroad and is fully occupied with outreach and/or Bible teaching.

3
J Nam's story

I was born and grew up in a very large family in a country village in South Korea. Buddhism is the traditional religion of Korea but our family was more influenced by Confucianism which emphasises moral living and especially honouring one's parents in this life and after death. There was a church behind my primary school, but I never went there and it wasn't until I was about ten years old that I even heard the name of Jesus.

My friend's father was accidentally killed while he was trying to stop a fight between two young men. At that time the offender would normally be imprisoned for life but my friend's mother publicly forgave him and the sentence was reduced to 15 years. I heard that she had forgiven him because she loved Jesus. Who is this Jesus, I wondered? As far as I was concerned, if someone had killed my father, I would kill him!

During my teens my physics teacher impressed me by the way he treated our class. He was always smiling and never got angry, even though we behaved mischievously at times. I found out that he was a Christian when a friend told me she had seen him carrying a large Bible as he went into church. I said to myself that when I grew up, I'd like to have a Christian family. Around this time, I sneaked into a marquee where many boys from my brother's mission school were watching *Quo Vadis*, a film with a Christian theme. I was impressed by a scene where Paul was going to Rome. I became more curious about Christianity and later I attended a church for about a year when I was at High School. However, I couldn't believe the resurrection. This was mainly because when my grandfather had died (I was about 11) he didn't come back and so I thought that life ended when we die and so for Jesus to come back to life was impossible.

After High School, I went to UNS university nursing school where

I joined UBF (University Bible Study Fellowship) for a short time to improve my English – they used an English Bible to study the Bible. However, from around this time I began to think that there must be only one truth in the world and I read a few philosophical books, but couldn't find any satisfying answers there.

Jea-Nam with one of her nieces, at graduation in 1973

    I also became interested in working abroad and soon after finishing nursing training I went to work in West Germany. The following year a Christian friend invited me to a Korean Christian conference in Switzerland. The main reason I accepted was to see the beautiful Alps, but when I got there, I felt out of place. I wanted to go back home, but this wasn't possible because there was no means of transport. I felt frustrated, but at the same time I was overwhelmed by the beauty of unspoiled nature, especially the wild autumn flowers. In these surroundings I felt for the first time that my heart was not clean.

I went along to the conference meetings simply because there was nothing else to do, but in one message the speaker talked about John 1:4, *"In him (Jesus) was life, and in him was the light of men."* There was like a sudden flash of revelation in my heart – if Jesus hadn't been resurrected, He couldn't have been the light of men. Suddenly I was convinced that Jesus had been resurrected and that He is the truth. The conference ended and I started studying the Bible. Three months later I admitted I had ignored God for 26 years, repented, and experienced His love and forgiveness.

One-and-a-half years later I moved to West Berlin and started attending an Assemblies of God church. There I was challenged about having a deeper relationship with the living God and at a special Easter service God graciously poured out His Spirit on me. I had a tremendous sense of peace and joy and received the gift of tongues. I also had a strong desire to know the Bible better and to share the gospel. At this time, I was also healed from severe back pain as a result of receiving prayer. From then on, I realised that supernatural healing was not just something that happened in the Bible.

A couple of years later, having attended Bible college (while working), I went to London to improve my English at Abbey School, a Christian EFL (English as a Foreign Language) school. I felt called to be a missionary and considered English would be essential. I assumed I'd probably serve in Africa, especially after a Korean friend had gone to serve in Africa, but God was to have different plans for me.

4
Japan, not Africa

J NAM went to Bible College again, this time in Belgium she continues her story. One day, while in prayer, I became aware that my heart was not for Africa but somewhere in Asia. I went back to Abbey School and continued to study English while working for the school as an "au-pair". Here I met Roger, who was a new teacher on the staff. He had spent some time in Japan and was eager to go back. At first, I thought it'd be best if he found a Japanese girl to marry and go back quickly to Japan! However, we got to know each other quite well and after a while became fond of each other. Then the opportunity came about for Roger to return to Japan and we had to consider our future. Parting was very hard but at least we could write to each other and occasionally telephone.

Roger with English class students, Abbey School, 1987

Meanwhile I had to make sure of my personal calling as a missionary. This came about when I was having a personal time of prayer and I sensed the Lord say, "Are you willing even to go to your enemy's country?" This confused me because I saw the 'enemy' as North Korea, but I soon realised God was speaking of Japan. I answered, "Yes, Lord. I am willing." That didn't automatically mean that Roger and I would get married, though.

After finishing at LBC in 1987 I, Roger, had found a job at Abbey School. I enjoyed working there, but more significant was that it was there I met J Nam. But when the opportunity arose for me to teach English in a Christian language school in Kobe, Japan I felt it was right to take it and J Nam agreed, even though it was very painful for us to separate. So it was that we carried on a long-distance relationship and became engaged over the phone in December. International phone calls were much more expensive in those days!

J Nam came to see me in Kobe – her first ever visit to Japan – and together we visited Korea to meet her many relatives. I had been concerned that, in view of Japan's oppressive colonial rule of Korea (1910-45), they might be hostile to our plan of going to Japan, but was relieved that my fears turned out to be unfounded. I was warmly welcomed even though I only knew no more than a few words in Korean and very few of them spoke much English. Later J Nam told me that one of her uncles had studied in Japan when Korea was a Japanese colony and that her father had also wanted to study there. His father hadn't allowed him to go, saying that it was enough for one son to go to Japan! J Nam's father was somewhat concerned that, as we were planning to be missionaries, we would never be affluent, but, although he wasn't a Christian, he urged us "to serve your God wholeheartedly".

Marriage

A few months later in August 1989, on a lovely summer's day, we were married at Abbey Road Baptist Church, London. J Nam was very pleased her father approved of Roger. Even though he and other relatives were unable to come to our wedding he showed his support by paying for our reception at a beautiful place near Regent's Park.

Wedding day with Roger's parents 19th August 1989

After marriage we moved into a small flat – or rather a large room – (sharing a kitchen and bathroom with others) right next to the church. I was able to resume my job at Abbey School, while J Nam continued her job, though part-time, as a nurse at Mildmay Mission Hospital. Sensing God's call to return to Japan, we soon began investigating how we might serve the Lord as missionaries. As part of this we attended an excellent weekend event put on by a missionary society for those with an interest in joining them. One result was that we were told we'd need at least another year of Bible college. We applied to All Nations Christian College (ANCC) as we were attracted by the emphasis on cross-cultural preparation.

We were accepted for the two-year course starting in September 1991. Finances were a challenge, but God provided - mainly through J Nam getting a LEA grant. By the time we finished we felt the LORD was leading us to serve Him with OMF International. Part of that guidance was through meeting Ray Porter who had recently started as the East Region director. We were among his earliest recruits to OMF and the very first for Japan. Ever since we have much appreciated his encouragement and input into our lives.

While at ANCC, even more significant than our developing relationship with OMF, was the birth of our lovely daughter, Angela. J Nam had prayed for her to be born two weeks early, before the second year started and this prayer was answered. However, she'd forgotten about the prayer and so we were unprepared when it began to be apparent that baby had decided it was time to come into the world! Having a child was later to lead to some new challenges to our cross-cultural marriage.

5
Further hurdles to overcome

ALL NATIONS had excellent crèche facilities and this meant that J Nam was able to continue studying and so finish her course. During this time something occurred which could have ended our plans of going to Japan. When Angela was about three months old our tutor told us that the crèche's staff were concerned that her hearing didn't seem to be normal. J Nam then recalled that her sister-in-law had said something similar at Christmas. We decided to make a test. With Angela sitting on the floor and facing J Nam I crept up behind her and loudly bashed a saucepan with its lid a few times. She didn't respond at all! We can still remember the terrible shock we felt then. But as it was Friday afternoon, we couldn't see a doctor until the following Monday. After some tests a nurse confirmed that there was some abnormality but as Angela was so young another test was needed nine months later. That gave us a ray of hope and then, as time passed, we noticed she was responding. We continued with our studies and when the second test was conducted, we were relieved that the results were normal. We still don't know what happened then, whether God directly answered our prayers for healing, or if it were just a natural development.

We finished at All Nations Christian College (ANCC) in July 1993. Our application to join OMF was ongoing and we had lots of forms (did OMF mean One More Form?!) to fill in and were interviewed several times. At the final interview we were ushered into a large room to meet the council, a group of several older, grave-looking personnel. We were sure what they would first ask us as when we'd finished our courses at ANCC we were unable to pay the fees for our final term. The chairman of the council wanted to know what we proposed to do about the debt? We couldn't join OMF and go overseas owing a large sum of money. We were able to tell them that funds were coming soon!

J Nam had asked her eldest sister to send some money of ours that was in Korea. It was about £500; very helpful but not enough. Around midnight on the day before our interview her sister phoned to say that another sister was going to send £3,000! Apparently, she'd done very well with some stocks and shares. When we shared this there was rejoicing all round and thanks to God for His wonderful provision. None of the council members looked very grave any more.

The final stage, some months later, would be to attend a Candidates Course. Meanwhile, as it would be some time before we could go to Japan, we moved to north London and I found some English teaching.

Around this time my father went into hospital for major surgery. It was clear that he felt he might not survive it and on one of our visits to him he was distinctly more open to the Good News of Jesus than usual. Sensing this, J Nam asked him if he was sure of going to Heaven. Could he ask Jesus to be his Saviour? We were surprised when he replied, "Yes. I'll do it right now" and we helped him to make a prayer of commitment using a tract I had with me. That evening, when my mother visited him, he told her, "I'm now a confirmed Christian."

A couple of months after this, we heard that J Nam's father was seriously ill with cancer and didn't have long to live. We went to see him in South Korea as soon as we could, staying in the family home in a small country village. J Nam was able to spend about three weeks with him caring for him, but more than this God gave us the great privilege of leading him to pray to receive Jesus as his Saviour, only a few days before he passed away.

'Extraordinary candidates'
Back from Korea in early January 1994 we almost immediately joined around 10 others for an OMF Candidates Course at Sevenoaks. On the last day we felt both relief and excitement when the Home Director, David Ellis, told us that we'd been accepted as future workers for Japan. We were designated as 'extraordinary candidates' because we were past the age limit for new workers. It was thought that if you were over 35 you would find learning the language too difficult.

However, exceptions were made for us because I had already learned some Japanese and J Nam's mother tongue, Korean, was closely related to Japanese.

Yet we still had to wait over a year before we could leave for Japan. I went back to teaching English, but then an unexpected opportunity arose. A Korean pastor J Nam had met invited us to spend some time in Korea. It was a great opportunity, we felt, and so we went back to Korea and for six months I taught English and did a little teaching about world mission; J Nam usually translating. Our daughter Angela had her second birthday and became fluent in Korean. When we returned to the UK in December my parents were surprised she spoke to them in Korean. It took a day or so before she understood that Daddy was not the only person in the world who didn't speak Korean!

1995

In January 1995 a major earthquake struck Kobe killing around 6,000 people. When I had lived there six years earlier the locals told me that they never had earthquakes. Anyone who plans to spend time in Japan needs to be aware that earthquakes can happen anywhere in the country. However, we had no hesitation in going ahead with our commissioning service which was held at Abbey Road Baptist Church, our local church at that time. Then at the end of February we went to the OMF national conference at Swanwick, Derbyshire, where on the Saturday night, with one or two others, we were interviewed as new OMFers. We flew from Heathrow the day after the conference ended to join an Orientation Course at the OMF International HQ in Singapore before going on to Japan. It had been an extremely cold day in England and we were hit by the steamy tropical heat when we landed.

At the Orientation Course in Singapore, we officially became members of OMF and felt we'd really arrived when we received, in Singaporean dollars, our first allowance. The six-week course was a valuable time, learning more about the mission and meeting the international leadership. We met a number of other new workers from various countries who were designated for various places in East Asia, including two American couples and a single British lady heading for Japan with us.

6
OMF missionaries in Japan – at last!

ABOUT two weeks before we left Singapore for Japan there was the very serious sarin gas attack on the Tokyo underground by members of the cult, Aum Shinrikyo. When we landed in Japan the country was still coming to terms with the shock of the attack and there was a suspicion of any minority religious group. No doubt this was why when the immigration officer saw my 'religious worker' visa at the passport control he asked if I had any connection with Aum Shinrikyo. I was taken aback by the question and, with some indignation, replied in the negative saying that I was a Christian and Christians were people of peace.

So, in April 1995 we arrived at last in Japan, exchanging the tropical weather of Singapore for the very early spring-time of Sapporo, Hokkaido, where the winter snow had not yet completely melted. For the next two years we were to focus on studying Japanese at the OMF Japanese Language Centre (JLC), learning Japanese culture and becoming familiar with OMF Japan while adjusting to daily life as a family. J Nam went for her language lessons in the morning while I attended in the afternoon. As I had previously spent three-and-a- half years in Japan this was more of a challenge for J Nam. She worked extremely hard to get to grips with the language. Although Korean and Japanese are related languages and have similar grammar there were times when she felt she wasn't making any progress.

In those early days when we spoke to cashiers in shops or to waiters in restaurants people looked at J Nam even though I did the speaking!

OMF Japanese Language Centre, Sapporo, Japan, May 1995. Demolished five years later.

I wasn't finding it easy, however. It was somewhat irritating to hear compliments from my teachers on how well I was doing when I knew that I wasn't yet back to the level I had attained when last in Japan. At the same time, we were looking after Angela. She appeared to have no problems in adjusting and made one or two friends but scarcely spoke a word of Japanese for the first year. She must have lost her Korean at this time. J Nam was very intent on learning Japanese and we felt that trying to keep a third language going for Angela would be too much. We have since sometimes wondered if perhaps we were wrong.

During our time at JLC we got to know fellow OMFers from different countries and the Japanese teachers and staff. We attended a local church, understanding almost nothing of the sermon but enjoying a simple lunch together with folk almost every Sunday. Angela joined the Sunday school. Yet with our limited Japanese it was virtually impossible to make any real relationships, though the pastor and a few others were kind and friendly. We sometimes felt rather useless, but teaching an English class on Sunday afternoons in our second year there enabled me to make some definite contribution to the ministry of the church.

7
Snow and slush

1996

STARTING that first winter in Sapporo we had to get used to almost four months of snow. We learned to walk and drive on snow and ice, or through slush when the temperatures moved a degree or two above zero. From mid-December clearing JLC's car park of snow was a regular occurrence and students took turns doing it using large plastic shovels and 'snow dumps' that you pushed. We envied people who had petrol-powered snow clearers and/or heated drains into which you could put the snow.

Angela at the Sapporo Snow Festival, February 1996

At first this was a novelty; the snow was beautiful and we always had a white Christmas. However, over the years, the long winters with the battle to keep the snow at bay and taking care not to slip became stressful and enervating. That wasn't the case with Angela, though. Like other children she had no difficulty walking and running on the snow and ice and, later, even having skiing lessons at school. In those early years we well remember going as a family to the Sapporo Snow Festival in early February and seeing the amazing ice sculptures. As temperatures usually stay below zero for days, we made sure we were well wrapped up.

Angela's first day at kindergarten, April 1996 – middle, red dress

There was a big day in April when Angela started at kindergarten - or nursery school. We were pleased that it was run by a church and the teachers were all kind and friendly. Naturally, we were a little anxious as to whether Angela would fit in. Would she have enough of the language? Would she be teased for being different? But our worries turned out to be groundless and we were thankful to God and for everyone who was praying for us at that time. She must have been gradually absorbing Japanese from television, church and daily life because soon it came pouring out of her. And with dark hair she blended in quite well with the other children.

Kindergarten was only the first step of Angela's education and OMF encouraged us (and all missionaries) to think long-term. There was the option of her going to boarding school at some point and we felt we had to give that at least some consideration. It was not appealing to us but we realised we needed to be open to the possibility of God leading us in that direction. There were Christian schools in Tokyo (American), the Philippines and India which had good reputations and the majority of – though not all – children of missionaries had had good experiences there. One day we mentioned the idea to Angela to see how she would respond. She was very definite, "Mummy and Daddy, never, ever send me to boarding school!" Angela never changed her mind and we never seriously considered boarding school again.

So, we settled into a daily pattern of life of studying Japanese and fellowship with other missionaries. We also enjoyed getting to know our teachers at JLC as fellow brothers and sisters in Christ. Our goal in learning the language – and culture – was to find our role of 'direct' ministry in the task of building the Kingdom of God in Japan. After two years at language school the rest of our initial four-year term was to be serving at a church under either a Japanese pastor or a senior missionary. As we began to think and pray about exactly where that assignment might be it was agreed with the OMF leadership that a visit to the Greater Tokyo area in summer 1996 would be valuable, especially as J Nam had never been there. The population was over 33 million then. In 2023, at close on 38 million, it was the largest metropolitan area in the world. A programme of churches to visit and other appointments was made for us, but a few weeks or so beforehand it had to be cancelled. It was clear that J Nam was not in a fit state to go. She was very weak and tired; exhaustion from the stress of over exertion in language learning was probably the main cause as well as a thyroid problem. She needed a rest in a quiet place not a hyper-busy time traversing the most highly populated metropolis in the world. So instead, we went to stay at the OMF holiday home in a tiny village right by the sea in a remote part of Hokkaido. It was another world from the seething crowds of Tokyo and made for a quiet and restful time for us all.

One Sunday we went to church about five miles away. Knowing how few Christians there were in Japan, we didn't expect many to be there, especially in a small country town. Perhaps around ten people, I mentally calculated. To our surprise the three of us quadrupled the congregation.

After our holiday, back in Sapporo, J Nam resumed her language study, suitably refreshed. We never made a station visit to Tokyo.

8
Leading a Japanese church

1997

OMF missionaries are not told where they will be sent, rather the missionary and leaders discern the Lord's purposes together. We appreciated this policy and, while open to go anywhere, expressed a preference to stay in Hokkaido. At one point there was the possibility of serving under a Japanese pastor in the city of Kitami, more than four hours away. We made a station visit there (looking out for bears as we drove through the countryside) and were impressed by the work being done but it didn't feel quite the place for us. Another church in the suburbs of Sapporo was considered briefly but eventually it was arranged for us to serve under senior missionaries, Dale and Maude Viljoen, in the port city of Otaru, less than an hour by car from Sapporo. They were leaders of a congregation of about 20 or so regular attenders.

Dale and Maude were from South Africa and we got on well and still have occasional contact with Dale; sadly, Maude died of cancer several years later. We were almost exactly the same age but they had joined OMF much earlier in life while J Nam and I had joined later on in life. We started at Otaru Evangelical Church in early April, excited though also a little apprehensive (more me than J Nam) at the prospects ahead of us. This was because Dale and Maude were about to go on a short Home Assignment (HA) and we were to lead the church on our own for five months. We soon found out that Dale had prepared things very thoroughly for us. He had arranged for many guest preachers so that I only had to preach once a month. That was definitely enough for me as preparation took an extremely long time, partly at least because I was (and still am) somewhat of a perfectionist. Sermon preparation invariably finished after midnight on the Saturday. As our flat didn't have an office I worked in the pastor's office and had a short walk home up quite a steep hill in the dark, a walk that included cutting through a Buddhist graveyard. In August at the 'Obon' festival, offerings made to visiting ancestral spirits are left at graves. I remember seeing fruit, sweet dumplings, even cans of beer! The smell of incense lingered for several days.

A day or two after moving into our flat we had an interesting cultural experience. We decided to follow the Japanese custom of visiting our new neighbours (for us about eight flats up the stairway) to introduce ourselves. As we'd learned at JLC we took a small gift of soap and a face towel to each door. Most people were surprised and one person didn't seem to quite know what we were doing! Apparently, the custom was out-of-date – at least for these people. And we never got to know them. On another day I was surprised and puzzled when a man came up to me and said, "You've come back". He thought I was the German OMF missionary who had served in Otaru a few years earlier.

Apart from monthly sermons I took my turn leading services, helped prepare the weekly bulletin and taught three English classes (later increased to four) every Tuesday in the church. These classes were to make contacts outside the church and at the end of each class I taught a 15-minute Bible lesson. One other task assigned to me was organising and leading a small tracting team. Once a month on Sunday afternoons we went out with tracts (and sometimes ads for the church's English classes) and put them through the doors of houses in different areas near the church. J Nam's area of service was attending the weekly ladies' bible study group and after a while taking her turn in leading it. Once a month they had a cooking class which attracted a number of non-Christian attenders. J Nam also assisted in the very small Sunday school and, to become better equipped for children's work, went to Sapporo to take a course for half a day once a week. Eventually she gave the Bible talk at Sunday school once a month.

One ministry we did together was leading the young people's group. Occasionally we invited them to our flat. The members were not particularly young – one man was in his mid-forties – rather the criteria for joining were that you were still single. One 'youngish' lady, had been a member of the Moonies and we weren't sure about her faith. When J Nam started an individual Bible study with her it seemed she was still under the cult's influence. Eventually she left the church and sadly later joined a modern Buddhist group.

Angela went to the church's Sunday School and memorised the Bible verses they were given. We sometimes asked her what the verse meant in English after she'd recited it to us in Japanese. Angela's rendering of Acts 3:19 was, *"Don't pray to statues, and turn to God and worship Him, the real God."* We found a kindergarten for Angela that was run by a church in the city centre, three miles away, and that meant I had to drive her there and back almost every day. However, that proved to be an opportunity to develop the father-daughter relationship. We still remember the 'Foxhill Farm' stories I made up to entertain her during the rides. There was a kindergarten that was much closer to us, but it was run by a Buddhist temple. Angela was by now perfectly at home with speaking and listening in both Japanese and English and started going to a 'club' to begin learning how to read and write in Japanese. Meanwhile I helped her at home with the relevant skills in English. Later this became more systematic. Around this time, she started having piano lessons.

We enjoyed getting to know the pastor of the church which ran the kindergarten and his wife also. The kindergarten celebrated its 100th anniversary while Angela was there; it had been started by an American missionary lady and a small group from the church that had sent her visited for the event. I met Pastor Kitamura once a week for a time of language exchange and his wife joined J Nam on the course for children's work. It was sobering to learn that Pastor Kitamura's parents had been in Nagasaki on August 9 1945 when the second atom bomb was dropped. Being on the other side of a hill shielded them from much of its effects.

With Dale and Maude resuming church leadership after their Home Assignment we were free to visit the UK for a four week break over Christmas and the New Year. We stopped overnight at the OMF guest home in Ichikawa, near Tokyo, and despite it being a very cold night Angela encountered what must have been the last surviving mosquito of the year. The next morning her face had several red bites and blotches which took a few weeks before they disappeared – my family members were somewhat surprised by this. It was lovely to see them and others after being away for approaching three years.

1998

We also visited St Peter's church, Watford, for the first time. This was to be very important for us for the rest of our time in Japan – and beyond. The church had been looking for missionaries to focus support on and decided on us after Hilda Wigg, a recently retired missionary, spoke there one Sunday. She knew us well as she had been responsible for new missionaries during our first year in Japan. St Peter's had a link with Japan as one of the church leaders had a brother who had spent a few years there with OMF. The church seemed quite excited about linking up with us; the vicar said that meeting us was like an 'incarnation' and remarked how 'ordinary' we were. Perhaps they had unreal expectations about missionaries!

On our return to Japan, we had to transit Tokyo which meant taking a coach from one airport to another. There was plenty of time – we thought – but we hadn't bargained for heavy snow in Tokyo which was rare and slowed us down considerably. We were just in time to catch the last flight to Sapporo and almost the very last passengers to board the plane. Once we got back to Sapporo there was far more snow, but they were used to it and so there was no problem getting a train back to Otaru and then a taxi home.

For the next few months life continued happily in a regular pattern as we served in the church under the Viljoens and aimed at sharing the love of Christ with non-Christians. There were a number of 'seekers' linked with the church and one of them lived almost next door to us. One day this lady told J Nam that she had come to believe in Jesus as her Saviour and a couple of months later she was baptised. Her husband said he would definitely not attend the service, but on the day he dropped into the church about half-way through, just to see the baptism. A widower was also baptised. There had been a memorial service about six months earlier on the first year anniversary of the death of his wife. Over 50 had attended –about three times the size of the congregation – and her testimony had been read out, expressing the peace she'd found through believing in Christ. Around this time the church arranged a special children's outreach and at the main meeting Angela took a step forward to show that she wanted a clean heart. It was a significant time for her.

Children's Outreach

Then something very unexpected happened. We were asked by the OMF Hokkaido leader, Wolfgang Langhans, if we would consider moving to another church. Actually, about two to three weeks earlier we'd heard at the OMF missionaries' weekly prayer meeting that there was a need to lead a church in Sapporo whose pastor had resigned.

It never occurred to us that we might be asked to fill that need yet as we drove home that evening J Nam began to wonder if we might be called upon and so when the request came, she wasn't greatly surprised. However, she wondered if our language would be adequate as we were only in our first term. For me thoughts like, "Surely someone else would be better" immediately came to mind. And we both felt, "What? Move again so soon!" We'd only been in Otaru just over a year. Wolfgang admitted there was another person he could ask if it were really necessary but he didn't want to. So, we agreed to pray about it. Two weeks later we were ready with our answer. Yes, we would take on the leadership of the church in Atsubetsu, SE Sapporo. The start date was in about three months' time, at the end of August. We were sad to leave Otaru but excited (and a bit apprehensive) at the new challenge we would face. For Angela it meant separation from a very close friend from the kindergarten. Yet they were able to meet from time to time – mainly because J Nam had become friends with her mother, who was Korean. Angela and her friend are still in touch more than 25 years later.

Before moving back to Sapporo, we went to Korea for our summer holiday. We hadn't been there for getting on for four years. It was good to see J Nam's many sisters and other relatives, though, to be honest, sometimes tiring for us both. Soon after getting back to Japan, we

Angela outside the family home in South Korea.

moved into the house which also served as the church building for Atsubetsu Evangelical Christ Church. Upstairs there was a room that served as an office, a toilet and a long room that could be divided by a concertina wall to make two bedrooms. Downstairs was another toilet, a Japanese-style bathroom with two washbasins and an open plan living and dining area with a kitchen. We had this all for ourselves except for when a mid-week church activity was held and on Sundays when there was the service and a time of fellowship. Every Saturday we had to prepare downstairs by putting away Angela's toys, moving furniture, vacuuming and setting chairs out. We did this in the evening and J Nam usually ended up doing most of it and found it very tiring as I was finishing off my sermon preparation.

Sundays were always long but the atmosphere of the church was warm and family-like. Fellowship after the service was not having a cup of coffee but (as was the practice of almost every church in our denomination) having lunch together. This was usually a bowl of noodles and perhaps some fruit. This was followed by some kind of meeting or free time during which most folk were in no hurry to go home and if they did leave 'early' usually apologised. The long Sundays were good for practising our Japanese and getting to know the very small congregation of about 10 people. Yet having our living place 'taken over' every Sunday did sometimes become quite wearing, especially for J Nam. Later, when we moved out to a nearby flat, it became easier.

Angela had to move to a new kindergarten and again we found one run by a church. This time the kindergarten was quite near (but not the church) so I usually took Angela there and back on my bicycle. At their Christmas party I was asked to dress up as Santa Claus at which I told the children not to forget that Christmas was about Jesus.

Sometime after this we faced a challenge regarding a Shinto ritual at a festival which celebrates the arrival of spring. It was called 'mame-maki' (bean throwing), and was supposed to ward off evil spirits. We were surprised that the kindergarten also had a mame-maki event and were uneasy about Angela participating. We didn't want her to stand out as possibly the only child not involved but more important, we felt, was that the atmosphere and Shinto-based meaning could be harmful. No doubt most Japanese see such things only as having fun while following an old tradition. In the end, when she heard about what was involved, Angela herself didn't want to join in. How to respond to Japanese cultural events is often a challenge for missionaries and their families and indeed for all Christians in Japan.

At our church there was only one other child and no Sunday school. However, Angela liked the church partly because some of the adults played with her on Sundays. After a while we started a children's club (which we named "Fruits Kids") every other Saturday afternoon. Most of the kids who came were Angela's friends from her new kindergarten and later from her school. A young Japanese lady, Kaori, worked with J Nam in running Fruits Kids. We already knew her since I had become friends with her American husband a few years earlier at the OMF Japanese Language Centre. Bill worked as an English teacher and before we came to Atsubetsu they had started a church English class. They both had musical gifts which they used in Sunday worship. Both J Nam and I very much valued our fellowship with them; this was especially so for me as it meant an opportunity to speak freely in English! Bill appreciated it too. On one or two occasions we did open-air outreach together at a nearby shopping centre. He played his guitar and I gave out tracts.

Challenges and encouragements

The area of Atsubetsu had a reputation for having large numbers of 'new' religious groups. It wasn't so long before we saw that for ourselves. A few minutes' walk from our church' was a massive building for 'Reiha no Hikari' ("Spiritual waves of light") which we later discovered was the centre for all of Hokkaido. We often noticed people in white gowns sweeping their courtyard and side streets. Not much further away was a large Mormon temple and then there were Jehovah's Witnesses who were active from their hall nearby. A member of the Unification Church was living locally and later we noticed their building. Yet another group, called "Happy Science", had many books by their founder and leader in a local bookstore. When our reading of Japanese improved enough, we noticed that a large building was the site of a popular modern Buddhist sect. It was called a church! As well as these 'new religions' there was also a traditional

Shinto shrine just along the road. This all heightened our sense of being involved in spiritual warfare. Apart from our church there were a few other churches and we eventually made contact with most of them. The leaders sometimes got together for prayer. Some churches were not evangelical.

Atsubetsu Church was small – even for Japanese churches – and had gone through a difficult period with declining numbers before the pastor had resigned. We concluded that our initial priority was for the members to be revitalised in their relationships with God. We believed that through this they would be encouraged and then emboldened to reach out to those around them. Exactly how we would see this goal achieved was a key question to which we weren't sure of the answer.

Funeral of Kudo Kaneko, 1999

We prayed, the two of us and with church members and we asked for prayer from fellow OMF missionaries and in our prayer news bulletins to our prayer partners in the UK. We often had a sense of being supported and guided by God in response to the prayers of others.

Preaching was a major way of ministering to the church, particularly as some church folk only attended on Sundays. This was a challenge for me as I had to go from speaking once a month to three times a month. For the other Sunday we found guest speakers, usually

Japanese but occasionally OMF missionaries. I think it was during these early days at Atsubetsu that I began to alter my approach to preaching. When at language school I wrote out every single word, had it checked and corrected by the Japanese teacher and then read it out while struggling to attain clear pronunciation. Occasionally I glanced at the listeners, but only for a second or so in case I lost my place. For the church congregation, hearing a foreigner speaking Japanese had some novelty, but this probably didn't last very long. I came to sense that my sermons were stilted and it wasn't very long until a few people began to find it difficult to concentrate, even nodding off. Most continued to listen, whether out of politeness or curiosity or a hunger to get some spiritual nourishment.

I came to see the need to make my sermon delivery more spontaneous. I did this firstly by writing in my sermon manuscript one or two notes for myself such as, "speak briefly about love" or "explain the Cross" or whatever. In this way there was a brief period of face-to-face contact with the congregation. It clearly had an impact and it was amazing to see people respond positively by showing more interest or even, in some cases waking up from their nap! With this encouragement I more and more developed the practice of speaking only from notes (a mixture of English and Japanese) though often writing out a sentence or two in Japanese or when I had to explain something difficult.

Preaching continued always to be a challenge throughout our time in Japan – and beyond – though it got a little easier over the years. Occasionally I wondered if I was spending too much time in preparation as I always finished very late on Saturday evening – or even in the small hours of Sunday. I developed the habit of praying in tongues as a vital part in preparing my mind and heart; this assisted me in the spiritual conflict I was involved in. Quite often I had the feeling on Saturday night that what I'd prepared was useless, that I had nothing of value to bring to the congregation, but almost always God brought me through to a breakthrough. And if nothing else I always felt that at least I myself had been blessed by all the effort to produce a message!

In addition to prayer and preaching, a third way of ministering to the church was developing close and warm relationships with the members, corporately and with individuals. Almost everyone was open to this, though there were one or two who appeared to hold back. Perhaps we tried to move too quickly or were too western in our approach, though J Nam is Korean. There was time on Sunday afternoons for interaction with church folk; sometimes a study time, sometimes walks in the park. We also inherited a monthly home meeting, which consisted of Bible study followed by lunch, at the home of one of the church members. In all cases this challenged and improved our Japanese language ability, especially in the area of listening. At the end of December, it was encouraging to receive a fax from a church member thanking us for coming to Atsubetsu and saying that there was a new wind blowing in the church.

Although our focus was on strengthening the church we didn't ignore outreach. This was carried on mainly through English classes, and the Fruits Kids ministry which opened the door to meet mums and sometimes dads and other family members. Together with church folk we distributed tracts in nearby blocks of flats. J Nam and I also visited

Atsubetsu Church English class

lapsed church attenders and were encouraged when one lady returned. At Christmas there were the special opportunities for evangelism and, as in Otaru, it was always a white Christmas. Japanese are familiar with ku-ree-su-masu, but extremely few know its true meaning – even less than the average Brit. A typical Japanese Christmas involves Santa Claus, decorations, Christmas music in department stores, fried chicken, family gatherings with a cake and for young people a special date with one's boy or girl friend on December 24th. We focused on explaining the true meaning of Christmas at our English classes, Fruits Kids meetings and a Christmas Eve service followed by food. We gave everyone suitable literature.

Christmas finishes on 24 and December 25 is a normal working day and so churches have nothing on. That was when we had our family Christmas, often meeting with other missionaries for the day. After Christmas there was some time to rest a bit, but then came the New Year celebrations which are much more important for Japanese. December 31 has Buddhist associations while on January 1st, 2nd and 3rd great numbers visit Shinto shrines. As with many churches we had a special service and lunch together on January 1st.

1999

During the three months after Christmas there was less outreach as winter slowed things down. Just clearing the church car-park of snow took up quite some time and energy. I remember having to dump much of the snow about 50 metres away by a small river. Fortunately, this was usually with the help of one or two church members. Winter temperatures fell to levels we weren't used to in the UK and we had to learn to turn off the water at night when the temperature got to around minus 8C. When we were no longer living in the church building, we had to be particularly careful on Sundays because Monday was a day off. On one occasion we forgot to turn off the water and on the Tuesday morning after the heating had been on a while we encountered a burst pipe in the bathroom.

Around this time an extremely large support gift which came from a supporting couple in the UK was a tremendous encouragement. This was especially so for J Nam as she had been going through a phase of feeling very down. She'd found herself wondering why she was in Japan because nothing seemed to be happening at the church. The gift helped to wake her up from this negative way of thinking and gave fresh strength to serve the Lord at Atsubetsu church.

Once winter was over that year a big day arrived for us when Angela started school (the school year in Japan starts in April). As far as we knew she was the only non-Japanese in the school, but she settled in well and with her dark hair was not conspicuous (children with blonde or fair hair find it harder). The local primary school was only about a five-minute walk away so that before long she walked there and back without us, often with one or two friends. There was little if any idea that children needed to be escorted to school.

Atsubetsu Church (in background) with our car

9
Home Assignment

1999-2000

WE ARRIVED at Heathrow Airport in early August 1999 for our first Home Assignment (HA). The OMF regional rep, Ray Porter, had found a flat for us to live in for the year. Soon after moving in we visited my parents in Southampton and it was great to see them every few weeks or so during the year. Later I realised more how it must have been hard for them not to see Angela growing up. One of the purposes of HA is to have time to reconnect with relatives, friends and church. For a number of reasons, it was better for us to live in Watford rather than in central London near the small church that had originally sent us out. St Peter's Church, which had 'adopted' us about 18 months earlier, warmly welcomed us and we quickly felt part of the church and local community. We much appreciated being invited by the vicar, Chris Cottee, to join the weekly church leaders team meeting. We were also pleased to be given the opportunity to share about our Japan work and I occasionally preached. As well as this Chris took me along to meetings of local church leaders. There were some Sundays when we spoke at other churches as part of our OMF deputation (as they called it then) but usually we were at St Peter's.

Visiting and sharing at OMF prayer meetings took place on weekdays and day conferences were on Saturdays. We were thankful that a place at a good school near the church was found for Angela and she settled in quite well. In the first few days some of her classmates were curious about her packed lunch of rice balls, but she soon asked to have sandwiches like everyone else.

In early November there was a great shock when the school burnt down because of an electrical fault. Fortunately, nobody was in the building as the fire started at around 6am. The children were happy that the school's goldfish survived! For the rest of the school year classes were held in Portacabins and everything seemed to go well.

One important thing we needed to do was to find a way to keep Angela's Japanese going. Given the right circumstances children can easily and naturally pick up a foreign language up to the age of around eleven. But they can easily lose it too. Angela was at native level when we left Japan, but we knew that she would very likely lose it if she had no opportunity to use it. Although we sometimes spoke in Japanese at home – usually just Angela and J Nam – we knew she needed more than that. The solution was to take her to a Japanese Saturday school in Finchley, North London. The school was for Japanese children who attended UK state schools during the week. It was only half a day, but with homework we felt it would be enough for Angela in our year away from Japan.

10
Back to Japan

2000

BEFORE we went back to Japan it was confirmed that we would continue to lead the church in Atsubetsu. About a month or so before the return date we were a little concerned to notice that Angela's Japanese was beginning to slip a little. However, once we were back in Japan it took only a day or so before she was completely at home in Japanese again. In fact, we came to face the opposite challenge, keeping her English going. To deal with this we made a rule that when she arrived home from school, after greeting us, we would speak only English, unless we had a Japanese visitor. The rule would have been harder to keep if Angela had not been an only child as siblings tend to chat with each other in the language they use at school. I started doing some home-schooling with her in English reading and writing and later some British history and geography. We had looked into this when in Britain and, following advice from OMF home-staff, started using materials sent from the UK.

With Mr Yamaguchi (plastic models of dishes on the menu)

Arriving back at the beginning of August we were warmly welcomed by the church folk. An elderly couple who lived opposite the church also welcomed us back. They were very friendly and once or twice, when we were delayed from getting home on time, they kindly allowed Angela to stay with them when she got home from school. It was a pity that, although we occasionally dropped in to see them and had some opportunities to share something of the gospel with them, they never came to anything at church.

While we'd been away an OMF missionary, Helen Lyttle, had lived in the church building and led some of the events as well as being there for the Sunday services. We were pleased to see how she had kept things going and that there were even a few new people coming on Sundays. There was an older couple from another church (the wife was a believer) who had moved into the area and there was a young man, Mr Imai, who had already done some beginners' Bible study with a fellow OMF missionary. I was able quite naturally to continue this. He had a Christian girl-friend going to another church, who was having a strong Christian influence on him.

At first, we lived in the church building but looked for new accommodation elsewhere. Meanwhile we went to the OMF Japanese language centre one day a week to attend a language refresher course. Finding a new place to live took longer than we'd expected but in mid-October we found a flat about a five-minute walk from the church. We prayed we'd be able to move in before the snow came; usually there was a little in early November but that year the very next day after moving in a few snowflakes fell.

After a while we decided to start another English class. We also began to pray for non-Christian male contacts and in looking for someone to print our flyers for the English class we met Mr Yamaguchi, who had his own small printing and publishing company. When Roger invited him into the building, he didn't believe it was a church! It's likely that his image of churches was only of larger purpose-built buildings with stained glass windows! This was the start of a relationship which continued throughout the rest of our years in Japan and beyond. I began to meet him for lunch during which eventually there were opportunities to read and share from the Bible. He came to church once in a while and even occasionally attended evangelistic events. Mr Yamaguchi was always keen to see me even after we left Atsubetsu and also whenever we visited Japan after returning to the UK in 2009. Some contact online continued and at the time of writing it's mainly by Facebook.

2001

After some months Mr Imai put his faith in Jesus and, after baptismal preparation lessons with me we had the joy of his baptism – our first in Japan! We used an old bath-tub.

Another first for us around this time was a funeral. An elderly church member who lived in a care home (we'd occasionally visited her on Sunday afternoons with a few church members) passed away. I'd had no involvement with a funeral in Britain, let alone in Japan but fortunately the previous pastor of the church kindly offered to conduct the funeral. We had some contact with him because his daughter had stayed on as an active member of our church. He suggested I give a short message just after the cremation and for three minutes a talk I'd prepared was duly delivered. Later he gently told me that he didn't mean a talk that short!

A more serious misunderstanding emerged with a church member who was, we later discovered, comparing us negatively with some other missionaries. At first, we couldn't understand what was happening as he spoke of the need for more 'harmony' in the church. We had thought there was quite a harmonious atmosphere, but now we sensed some tension with him. Then one Sunday afternoon the issue came out into the open as he surprised us by pouring out his thoughts and feelings about us, such as we were not very loving. We scarcely said a word in response (partly because we couldn't understand much of what was said!) and strongly resisted the urge to defend ourselves. "Roger, keep your mouth shut", I remember repeating to myself. J Nam was in floods of tears.

Thereafter to our amazement, all the tension almost immediately dissolved and from then on, his attitude towards us changed completely. We enjoyed good fellowship with him and he supported us in all we did in the church. God changed a negative situation into something positive though we never entirely got to the bottom of the initial problem.

From time to time, we met new people and around spring-time J Nam was introduced to a young mother by a church member who knew her mother. Chie had two small children and was suffering from deep depression. She had attempted to commit suicide more than once. J Nam started meeting with her in the church building on weekdays and spent hours listening to her story and little by little gained her trust. She also met her mother through a pottery group. There was gradual improvement in Chie's condition and she became open to one-to-one Bible study. Her children started coming to our 'Fruits Kids' children's meetings. Later she began to come to church on Sundays, usually with her husband. Around a year or so later she did some baptismal preparation with me but rather abruptly stopped after a few sessions saying she didn't feel ready. We were somewhat disappointed, but in retrospect we saw that it was good she didn't go ahead without an assurance of faith in Christ.

Illness of a different kind impacted the life of another lady we were in contact with. J Nam had first met Yumi in 1999 as her son and Angela were attending the same kindergarten. As the relationship developed her children started attending 'Fruits Kids' meeting and she came along to the church's English class and to some other church events. Then out of the blue she was diagnosed with cancer. She was quickly and successfully operated on. During her time in hospital J Nam visited her and it wasn't long before she became serious about wanting to know about Christianity.

2002

YUMI was now a seeker (*kyoodohsha* = literally, 'seeking the way person') and started Bible study with J Nam and came regularly to church on Sundays. After a few months she put her faith in Christ. I then took her through baptismal classes and in summer 2002 she became the second person we baptised at Atsubetsu Church. As with the earlier baptism for some of the people who came - relatives mainly - it was probably their first ever attendance at a Christian church.

With Atsubetsu Church members

It was personal contact that resulted in meeting the person who became the third to be baptised. The three-year-old son of Chie spent a few days in hospital (in Japan people stay longer in hospital than in the UK) and during this time I visited him. There was only one bed in the ward. After greeting the mother, I gave her some food that J Nam had prepared and went to where the little boy was lying and after a few words prayed for him. Chie then introduced me to a good friend of hers who had been quietly waiting in the background. I had only been vaguely aware of her presence and after greeting her left the hospital. I was quite busy that week and didn't stay long. To me it seemed to have been a routine visit that church leaders make, but very soon after this J Nam heard from Chie that her friend, Morimi, wanted to meet her. It was soon apparent that she was very open to the Good News of Jesus. She had nearly zero knowledge of Christianity, probably less than any other person we had ever met and had perhaps never even heard of Jesus. What had sparked her interest was the very brief encounter with me at the hospital. She told J Nam that there was some kind of light around my face which had struck her. When J Nam shared with her Matthew 11:28, *"Come to me, all you who are weary and burdened, and I will give you rest."* the words really spoke to her heart. J Nam then started a Bible study with her and her journey to faith in Jesus was surprisingly a very smooth one. Morimi accepted everything, had no doubts and that autumn she gladly received baptism.

Furthermore, some weeks later she was reconciled to her ex-husband – we devised a short 're-marriage ceremony' for them both in the church. He also had extremely little, if any, knowledge of Christianity but occasionally showed his face at special church events and gradually got to know some people. However, he didn't respond to the Good News and sadly quite a few years later we heard that they had become separated again.

2003

As we entered 2003, we knew that we only had until the end of July before we would leave Atsubetsu and return to the UK for Home Assignment. OMF's goal, together with that of JECA (Japanese Evangelical Church Association) was for the church to have Japanese leadership before we left. In the process of finding a pastor we didn't actually have much of a role – that was mainly handled by our advisor pastor. As he was one of the JECA leaders in Hokkaido, he had quite a lot of contacts and influence. A candidate, Dr Yoshida, was selected and the church met him one Sunday when he preached and faced a question-and-answer session after lunch. The church voted to invite him to become their pastor and this was to happen in April. In terms of financial support, it was helpful for the small church that he would continue to work one day a week as a doctor. Looking back now we probably didn't do enough beforehand to prepare the church for the change of leadership. There were occasions when we reminded church members that we'd be leaving in summer 2003 but they didn't seem to take it in. Perhaps it was because we didn't make a formal announcement early enough.

Meanwhile God was bringing us into contact with more folk who went on to believe and were baptised. One of these was in a group that sang Black gospel songs, something that was (and apparently still is) popular mainly among non-Christians! The songs are almost always in English and rarely do the singers know the meaning of the words but most are interested if someone explains. J Nam went along to one of these gatherings to watch and listen and met a young mother. Not long after she came to a Sunday service with one or two friends. It wasn't long before she had Bible study with J Nam, believed and, after preparation, was baptised. Her husband also began to show a definite interest, though belief and baptism didn't come until after we'd left. They both wanted to dispose of their Shinto *'kami-dana'* (god-shelves). These are like miniature shrines and are usually fixed high up on the wall of living rooms or in offices. They had one at home and the other in the office of the small business they ran. Although we knew that many people had god-shelves this was the first time for us to face the question of exactly what we should do when asked to help believers to deal with them. We asked for and followed the advice of our advisor pastor. He said it'd be best to ask the couple to give us the god-shelves and assure them that we would deal with them. I don't think we told them what we were going to do but, following the pastor's advice and with the help of a church member, we broke the god-shelves into pieces and put them into a large cardboard box. A few days later the box was put out to be taken away by the rubbish collectors.

There were two more baptisms before the new pastor came. One was the mother of Yumi, who we had baptised earlier and the other was Mrs Sawada, who had a severely handicapped son. J Nam had got to know her because she had been invited to join a Bible study that J Nam already had with an acquaintance of hers. As it happened the first lady never quite came through to faith but Mrs Sawada was spiritually open from the start – she'd been reading a New Testament given to her by a church kindergarten. After the two ladies came to faith in Jesus, I took them through baptismal preparation together and they were baptised at the same service. (Mrs Sawada had been concerned about whether she could afford to make a regular offering to the church but in the evening after her baptism she was able to quit her smoking habit and give the money saved to the church). It was a great time of praise and thanksgiving for us all in the church and very encouraging.

In our last few months, we also welcomed a few more people into church membership, one of them the fiancée of Mr Imai, who had been baptised in 2001. J Nam had been praying for 21 church members before we left Atsubetsu and this prayer was answered exactly!

We fitted in a visit to Korea before the new pastor was inducted in April. There then followed several weeks of leadership transition while the two of us shared the preaching. The little church building was nearly full on Sundays, partly because as well as the new pastor his wife and three children attended. The wedding of Mr and Mrs Imai took place and I was asked to officiate while the Pastor Yoshida gave the address. The whole event was carried out in the beautiful and spacious building of an OMF planted church in another part of Sapporo.

Centre of Sapporo

We knew we wouldn't be serving in the same place when we next came back to Japan and so the final day at the local primary school for Angela came. She'd had a good time at the school overall. We'd been impressed when her form teacher visited us to talk about how things were going. We remember her taking part in the sports day a few weeks before our departure. Apart from school she also said goodbye to a dance group she'd been involved with. J Nam had got to know the leader of the group who had attended the church's English class. Then our last Sunday came. It was great to have another baptism, which was conducted by Pastor Yoshida. A few days later, at the end of July, we made the one-hour flight to Tokyo from where, after a night in an airport hotel (which gave us a welcome breathing space), we flew for London. A total of four years ministry at Atsubetsu Church was over. Looking back, we had much for which to thank God.

11
Second Home Assignment
2003-2004

WE WERE back in Watford and once again the folk at St Peter's warmly welcomed us. This time Ray Porter had found us a house which was a five-minute walk from the church and about 30 seconds to the school gate for Angela. Having no need to drive Angela to school was to prove to be a great blessing over the year as, although we didn't know it then, I was going to be often visiting my parents in Southampton. The likelihood of that became apparent when, the day after arriving in Watford, on an extremely hot day, we drove down to see them. We were rather shocked at how Mum and Dad had aged. Only about a month later Dad had a fall and was hospitalised. He never lived at home again.

So it was that, while visiting churches, OMF prayer groups and other supporters as well as being involved with St Peter's Church, I drove to Southampton and back about once every three weeks. I saw Mum, walked the dog, went with Mum to see Dad in the community hospital and stayed overnight. J Nam and Angela came with me at half-term and during the school holidays. We had a memorable and somewhat poignant Christmas Day that year as Dad was allowed to come home for a few hours. J Nam prepared a lovely traditional Christmas lunch and we had some family time in the afternoon with one or two games including 'pin the tail on the donkey'. All too soon the time came to take Dad back. That night I had the strong feeling (which turned out to be right) that we'd had our last ever Christmas together with Mum and Dad.

2004

The visits to Southampton continued as our Home Assignment proceeded. Angela attended the Japanese school in London on

Saturday mornings as before. She also kept in touch with her friends in Japan by email. Clearly, she was keeping her Japanese going without any real problems and, perhaps because of this, Ray Porter suggested she take GCSE in Japanese before going back to Japan. This hadn't occurred to us but we found a school in London that offered Japanese GCSE and managed to get Angela entered to take the exam. It wasn't a surprise that she passed with an A* very easily. She finished the written paper early while the other, much older, candidates struggled on until time was up. The oral part of the exam was apparently little more than a casual chat with the Japanese examiner. The local newspaper heard about this and we had a journalist come to interview Angela and us which resulted in an article with Angela's photo.

My father died in April at the age of 86. It was on Maundy Thursday. Most of his life he'd had no interest in Christian things but he'd come to a personal faith in Christ in his mid-seventies. I was very thankful to be in the UK during my father's last few months on earth. The minister who led the funeral was one of Dad's cousins. On the way back to Watford that evening our car broke down – we were thankful it didn't happen going to the funeral.

About a month later we had a holiday by the sea in Wales. I hadn't got over my father's death and "somehow,' I became overcome by the strange sensation that I was soon to follow him. As I was in good health there was no rational reason for the way I felt, but somehow this nagging thought oppressed me and I couldn't shake it off. But then, three times in a single day, I happened to read the words, "*I shall not die…*"; in the Bible twice and once in a biography I was reading. I wasn't searching for such words; the Lord gave them to me and through them I was set free.

The time drew near for our return to Japan. My mother's health had been unstable for a few months. She was not finding it easy to manage despite having a daily carer, some help from church folk and regular visits from my brother and sister and their spouses. She'd also had a spell in hospital in March and again in May. In June and July she was getting better and it seemed that she was coping reasonably well. We decided to go back to Japan on schedule. I was glad that my brother and sister were around, though now in retrospect I probably took it too much for granted that they would accept our going back to Japan and expect them to look after Mum. Just before we flew a supporting couple kindly gave us a large amount to buy a new car for our use in Japan.

12
Opportunities and problems

WE had agreed to take over leading Tonden Christ Church in the NW suburbs of Sapporo. As in Atsubetsu it was extremely rare to see a Western person in the area. At first it was more common to see ostriches! There was an ostrich farm nearby and you could buy their eggs. About a year later, just as we seriously began to consider trying one, the farm suddenly closed down and we never saw any ostriches again. In the next four years we saw perhaps one or two westerners locally – there were more in downtown Sapporo.

The church situation was similar to what we'd faced at Atsubetsu. A church had been planted by OMF missionaries and a Japanese pastor had been appointed but after some years problems had been encountered, numbers had fallen and he had resigned. The church was struggling and members were mostly discouraged. What was different from Atsubetsu was that Tonden Church already had a lovely purpose-made building and there had been no pastor for over two years. The church folk appeared to be really relieved when we arrived and gave us a very warm welcome.

After a few days we found a flat only a five-minute walk from the church. We didn't spend much time trying to find out what exactly had gone wrong in the church in the past but focused on what we believed was God's purposes in the present. Our aim was to see the church re-planted and become spiritually healthy again, believing that thereby it would begin to grow again in all areas, including numbers.

Early on one active church member said to me that the church needed to get out and evangelise. Though I was pleased at his zeal I responded by saying that evangelism, though of vital importance, was not the church's number one priority right now. Rather it was healing and restoration within the church. The words in Isaiah 42:4, *"A bruised reed he will not break, and a smouldering wick he will not snuff out"* were given to us and stayed with us for the five years we led the church. We needed to care for those who were bruised and preserve the smouldering wick until the candle eventually began to burn brightly once more. So initially we focused on Sundays (service, lunch and fellowship) and a couple of mid-week meetings.

We started a day-time English class, which finished with a 10-15-minute Bible time, and a group of five or six middle-aged ladies from outside the church started coming. Later a retired man joined us. He had spent a few weeks in England and met a Christian couple who introduced him to us. We distributed tracts and flyers for the English class and started a Mums and toddlers' group. Some months later we started a children's outreach every other Saturday which was called Light-kids. J Nam and a church member were the leaders. Her teenage daughter, who became a good friend of Angela, was actively involved as was Angela.

A major change for Angela was that she started at Hokkaido International School (HIS). Based on our research and advice received we had decided that this time of entering secondary school was right for Angela to make the switch from Japanese schooling. The teaching at HIS was all in English but she was able to maintain her Japanese virtually at native level because she spoke to most of her friends in Japanese and took advanced level Japanese lessons. It was a longish journey each day as it was on the other side of Sapporo. I drove her to the nearest underground station and after a 22-minute journey it was a five-to-ten-minute walk to the school. On the way home for the last part of the journey she occasionally caught the bus. On Wednesday mornings I drove her all the way as I did a half-day at the school helping in the library. This wasn't proper voluntary work as we received a 25% reduction of school fees in return. On the whole Angela enjoyed her time at Hokkaido International School, made friends and still today has a very good friend from that time. As most of the teachers were American Angela gained a slight American accent. The curriculum was basically American so we had to bear that in mind when considering her future. To keep her awareness of British culture, I continued giving her home-schooling in British history and geography.

From HIS it wasn't very far to the church of our advisor pastor, who I visited every couple of months or so. It was always a valuable and encouraging time as it also was when he occasionally came to preach at Tonden.

Tonden Christ Church

In those early days at Tonden a church member who had stopped attending before we came visited us in our flat. We were surprised and sad to hear him say, "I will never forgive…" about an active church member. What the problem was exactly we never discovered but we became more aware of how vitally important forgiveness is in personal relationships and the functioning of a healthy, thriving church. After this there was an issue with a church member who appeared to be particularly discouraged and gloomy. At first, she had responded positively as J Nam sought to reach out in love to the ladies in the church. The two of them started meeting together and she became brighter. Then a couple of months later she abruptly began to behave strangely and became extremely negative towards J Nam. We couldn't find out why and tried to be conciliatory but she didn't change and it wasn't long after that she left the church. We were sorry about both people but it was also somewhat of a relief as they could have caused quite a lot of trouble in the church.

On a brighter note the year ended with Christmas events including one in which, for outreach, the church hired a local Chinese restaurant.

2005

A new thing for us was being asked by OMF leadership to have a younger missionary serve under us at the church. We were initially hesitant about this, perhaps mainly because I was unsure if I would be able to inspire confidence in the person who would join us. She was a single Korean lady and so there was the obvious connection with J Nam, though J Nam had not lived in Korea for many years. It can be quite lonely for singles in cross-cultural mission, the great majority are women and they benefit from having someone with whom they can have close fellowship in their mother tongue. This younger missionary had quite a lot of experience in outreach in Korea and Japan and spoke Japanese very well. Perhaps not surprisingly the three of us didn't always see eye-to-eye on everything in church life and to some extent we had to learn to adapt to each other. Nevertheless, we were fully united in our desire to reach out with the gospel and as part of this she started a Korean class. Like the English class this was held in the church building and included a Bible time at the end. Another contribution she made was arranging for a team of keen young Christians to come from a church in Korea for about a week of short-term mission. At that time Japanese were becoming more interested in Korea and the Korean language, mainly because of a very popular

Korean TV drama series. When she later moved on to serve in another church J Nam took over the Korean class; it was her first experience of teaching Korean.

J Nam with Angela outside Matsumoto Castle

Another new experience was being involved in a car crash. As I often did, I'd met Angela at the local underground station to give her a lift home. It was right at the end of winter and much of the snow had melted which made driving easier. I was feeling I could relax just a little – there seemed to be no longer any need for 100% total concentration. But only moments later at a junction I failed to stop and the crash happened! ("*So, if you think you are standing firm, be careful that you don't fall!.*" 1 Corinthians 10:12) The other driver was hurt but thankfully it wasn't serious, though he had to visit hospital a few times for whiplash, I think. At first, he was – understandably – very angry but when he found out that I was with OMF he calmed down noticeably. Apparently, he'd had quite a bit of contact with another OMF missionary who'd served at Tonden some years previously. The police were called (Angela helped with communication) and later I had to visit the police station two or three times. A church member helped me with filling in the forms for insurance matters; this taught us some new vocabulary. It was adjudged to be 95% my fault. Overall, although it was a stressful time, J Nam and I were grateful that the man concerned seemed to get over his injuries fairly quickly and no legal proceedings arose from the incident.

In August it was great that my brother with his wife and their two teenagers came to see us for nearly a week as a large part of their holiday in Japan. In Sapporo they stayed in accommodation owned by a church couple who kindly invited them and us over for supper. One day, when I mentioned that I was thinking of visiting my Mum that Christmas, my sister-in-law said that I should hurry up as she wasn't at all well. I was a bit shocked at this but later appreciated her plain-spokenness. Mum was then in a care home. I was in contact with her by phone and had thought she was all right but now realised things were otherwise. I hoped my planned Christmas visit wouldn't be too late but didn't think I could go any earlier. Then something happened to change my mind.

Westerners were a curiosity! (near our flat in Tonden)

One of my best friends was due to get married in mid-October. I didn't think I could afford to attend the wedding and then go to England again only a couple of months later. But J Nam came up with the obvious idea of going to England in October and do both.

My journey to London went via Hong Kong rather than Tokyo. The plane from Hong Kong left around midnight and as it was more than half empty, I was able to stretch out on three seats and get a good night's sleep. From Heathrow I caught a coach and arrived at my friend's house in Southampton at about 9am. Only a few hours later he gave me a lift to the care home to see my mum. She was pleased to see me but didn't look at all well and dropped off to sleep. The doctor happened to come at this time to examine her and after a very brief discussion I was able to persuade him to have mum taken to hospital.

Two days later I attended my friend's wedding and after a brief visit to our church in Watford I spent five days in Southampton, staying in my friend's house. So it was that God gifted me some time with my Mum as I made a short daily trip to see her. We didn't talk much, but I held her hand. I wasn't sure how clear her mind was at times but she seemed to appreciate it when I read a few verses from the Bible and prayed with and for her. It was difficult to tell how strong her faith was but the Lord keeps us even when we are weak. Leaving her at the end of my last visit to the hospital was sad and painful though I didn't know how much time she had left in this world. In fact, the very day after I got back to Sapporo a phone call came from my brother. Mum had just passed away.

I had little doubt about going back for the funeral. I wanted to be there and although there was the cost of the flight that was to be easily covered through money I would inherit. As well as this, I felt that not going would be a bad witness to Japanese folk, both Christian and non-Christian. Funerals are extremely important in Japanese culture and they are about the only reason someone is guaranteed to get time off work. So, I went back, for only three nights, I think. It was indeed a flying visit. I was pleased that my father's cousin, as for my father's funeral, kindly officiated at the funeral.

2006

In our work at Tonden Christ Church we continued to focus on developing a 'healthy' church while also desiring to see new people reached with the gospel. And 2006 saw the first person to believe. We had met a lady who lived locally when looking for piano lessons for Angela. (Angela became skilled enough to play at Sunday services once or twice a month.) She was quite friendly and open to talk and following an invitation from J Nam she began to come to Sunday services. After a while she started a one-to-one Bible study with J Nam and came through to faith quite quickly. I took her through baptismal preparation and after a session with two church members to assess if she were ready or not, she was baptised. It was a pity her husband didn't attend. It sounded like he was a workaholic, but her two young children did and began to become part of the church family. The baptism was a great encouragement for the whole church.

That summer we had another visitor from England, Chris Cottee, the vicar of St Peter's, Watford. We involved him in the life of the church as much as possible and he was keen to be involved. He joined our English class, our children's outreach meeting and preached once with me translating. At one point in the sermon, I gave a rather long explanation of the meaning of 'aura' but after the service a church member told me it's the same word in Japanese! As well as helping at our church Chris was the guest speaker at a youth group meeting in another Sapporo church. Another day I took him to visit the pastor of a country church that I knew quite well. Other memories were my showing him around a large Shinto shrine in the centre of Sapporo and, on another day, being surrounded by a group of curious schoolboys in the local park. Chris had a great time with us though he wasn't sure about some of the food! It was a very encouraging time for us too. Such visits by church leaders to mission workers and others overseas are usually very worthwhile.

That summer during a family holiday we had a new experience which was somewhat alarming. We'd set off to drive all along the coast to the far south-eastern extremity of Hokkaido. Our first stop was at a 'camp' to stay overnight in a log cabin. We wanted to go and see the coastal scenery but upon arrival in the late afternoon we were told to be very careful and not go far from our log cabin. Fresh droppings of a bear had been discovered in the vicinity. We certainly were very careful to comply with the directive! That night I even wondered if the cabin would be strong enough if a bear made a determined effort to get inside. Thankfully we heard nothing more about bears the next day nor for the rest of our holiday. The brown bears of Hokkaido occasionally go into country villages or even the edges of urban areas and can certainly be dangerous. Back then we never thought about bears where we lived but nowadays there are increasing numbers of sightings, even in the suburbs of Sapporo.

2007
Before long it was winter again but the novelty of the white scenery was dissipating. The experience of living in the snow and ice for more than three months became rather monotonous and tended to drain one's energy.

Clearing the snow in Tonden

In mid-January, with around ten weeks until the snow was due to melt, I quite often ended up with bouts of mild or moderate depression. J Nam didn't seem to be affected in this way. One day, during one of those periods when temperatures stayed below zero for more than a week, a revelation came to me. It was a time when nothing seemed to be happening at church and it was easy to slip into the negative attitude of wondering if 'our efforts' were achieving anything or were even appreciated. Such feelings are often symptomatic of depression and the devil loves to coax us into such negativity and false thinking. One day, as I was carefully walking home through the snow and ice, it occurred to me that even if the temperature rises by a few degrees there will be no noticeable change. Even with a rise from, say, –7 C to –4 C the ice will stay at hard as ever. In church life it can be the same. Spiritually things may be 'warming up' but no change is evident until we get above freezing point. So, what's the appropriate response? It must be to keep going, to patiently persevere by faith, trusting that God is at work and that in due time we'll get above zero and the ice will start to melt. As it says in Galatians 6:9, *"And do not grow weary in well doing for in due season we shall reap, if we do not lose heart."* By God's grace that year was to be our most fruitful year in terms of new believers, both in the church and our family.

On June 17th three people were baptised at the Sunday service, a very memorable occasion. Firstly, there was our 14-year-old daughter Angela. Six months earlier, at about 11.45pm on December 31st she'd had a vision while I was praying an 'end-of-year' blessing on her. In the vision she saw a cone-shaped hole which was her heart. From it her sins were taken out and the Cross was placed in her heart which caught any more sins from falling in. Then she saw a crowd outside a city wall and a book in which all her sins were written down. But then every sin was wiped away and assurance given that her name was written in the book of life. Also, God told her that He had a perfect plan for her life and said, "Do your part." This vision brought her to a definite personal faith. About a year earlier God had also spoken to her powerfully in Japanese, through Hebrews 2:14 which says that Jesus broke the power of sin, death and the Devil. This had set her free from the fear of death and also the fear of ghosts which had troubled her since her time at Japanese primary school.

Baptism of our daughter Angela in Tonden Church

The second person was Chie, the young mother who had pulled out of baptism at Atsubetsu a few years earlier. She'd recently started attending Tonden Church with her husband and two children and had come through to assurance of faith. The third person baptised was a retired man to whom we'd been introduced by the director and owner of a small local hospital who was a Christian. (One of our church members worked there part-time as a nurse.) He had been in this hospital for an operation and while there had found a Gideon's New Testament of the Bible which he'd started to read. This had led him to enquire about local churches. When we met him, we found that he had a degree of biblical knowledge because of some involvement with a Seventh-day Adventist Church about 25 years previously. I began a one-on-one Bible study with him but because of his very informal way of speaking I could hardly understand what he was saying and so soon realised I couldn't conduct the study unaided. I asked a church member to join us so that he could 'translate' whenever necessary and help to lead the study. I still remember this older man's amazement and relief that, because of God's grace, salvation is a free gift and only needs to be received by faith. It became apparent that at some time in his younger years he'd been involved in unlawful activity, possibly something similar to what the *yakuza* (Japanese gangsters) are known for. I never found out any more and didn't think it was necessary to probe any further.

The three people baptised in June 2007 just before the service started. Wearing white gowns for baptism is common in Japanese churches.

Sadly, his story in the end was not a 'success' as such – though ultimately only the Lord knows what goes on in a person's heart. He told us of the fierce opposition he faced to his faith from his wife. We never saw her at church, not even at his baptism and when we visited their house it was obvious that she was trying to avoid us – we scarcely caught a glimpse of her. Her antagonism was apparently relentless. On at least one occasion she threw away his Bible and on another, he told us, his clothes. Eventually he stopped coming to church and sadly we were unable to keep in contact with him.

That summer 2007 we made a short trip to the UK and Korea, partly because by then we'd committed ourselves to a five-year term. We visited Cambridge briefly as, following consultation with OMF, our plan from 2009 was to be involved in outreach to the many Japanese there. We also looked at two Sixth form colleges for Angela. One of them seemed ideal but there was no guarantee Angela would get a place, particularly as we weren't yet living in Cambridge. Over the next two years we kept in touch with the college by email.

After we got back to Japan, we felt led to use the Alpha Course which had been translated into Japanese. We'd thought and prayed about this for a while, discussed it with the church officers and sampled a session at a large JECA church. The church members agreed and so we decided to go ahead. We made a few changes, reduced the number of sessions and two topics were covered in Sunday sermons. Instead of the weekend away, which we felt very few if any would be able to commit to, we had a Saturday special instead. At this, I gave one of the three talks. We decided against advertising the course widely but focused on inviting our seeker contacts who already had some Biblical knowledge. After a brief trial run with church members, we launched out. It was generally well received and Yasunori the husband of Chie who was baptised in June, responded positively. Soon after, at a special evangelistic meeting at which Arthur Holland a half-Japanese, unorthodox 'motor-bike' evangelist came to speak, he came to faith in Jesus and was baptised before the end of the year. We ran another Alpha course in 2008 which also went well.

2008

The time was approaching to look for our successor at Tonden. We were due to finish in summer 2009 and would not be returning. A married man with two teenage sons, who was soon to graduate from the Hokkaido Bible Institute, was recommended. As an initial step J Nam and I visited him and his wife. The next thing was for them to meet us and the church officers together. At this point we found an area where expectations differed. He wanted his wife to be treated simply as an ordinary church member, but the church officers explained that they were looking for the pastor's wife to be active in church ministry, much as J Nam was doing. Later we felt this issue should have been clarified; it seems that both sides went away from the meeting thinking that eventually their point of view would prevail.

Church meeting, Tonden Church

The church members voted to accept him as assistant pastor for a year with the expectation that he would become pastor from Spring 2009. He joined us in April and at first things appeared to go quite smoothly. I spent time with him explaining our ministry approach, sharing the preaching on Sundays and showing him around the neighbourhood. Yet after a while it became evident that some of his ideas about church were different from ours. Furthermore, as he had initially told us, his wife took very much a backseat role as an 'ordinary' church member. As the church officers became aware of these things J Nam and I began to spend quite a lot of time with them talking about this and praying whether or not he was God's man for Tonden Church. All this discussion was a new experience for us – at Atsubetsu our successor was chosen and we had almost no say about the matter – and I found it rather stressful. I was glad to consult our advisor pastor as well as one or two senior OMF missionaries. Then a new and very serious factor was added to the situation; his wife was diagnosed with cancer. I remember the shock of receiving a text from him when our family was on a ferry coming back from our summer holiday. We saw little of her from then on, especially after she began to spend quite a lot of time at a healing centre in another part of Japan.

There was another sad happening around this time. A single man about the same age as me, unemployed, not in good health and with mental health issues was coming along to Sunday services quite often. He also dropped by at the church on weekdays from time to time as he was very lonely. On Sundays most people avoided him, especially the ladies.

One day his elderly mother died and the assistant pastor and I visited him in his small, untidy ground floor flat. We attended the funeral (Buddhist) and found that we were the only guests. There's a somewhat happier development to this story as he believed in Christ at another church. At the time of writing we are still in contact and he occasionally makes short phone calls to me. I also went to see him in his flat on one visit to Japan.

Church life overall continued to be encouraging and there were two baptisms in 2008. One of these was a young lady who'd had some connection with Tonden before we came. J Nam met with her and had many sessions listening to her life story. After a while they began to look at the Bible more and she came to put her faith in Christ. J Nam also got to know her mother well and after a while they started Bible study together. She showed a lot of interest and eventually believed and was baptised a year or two after we'd returned to England. The other person baptised in 2008 was wife of someone who had attended Tonden Church for a while before we came, and she did the Alpha course.

There were other ladies J Nam used her counselling skills with; some seekers and some church folk. She also gave some counselling to a man in the church. With everyone this usually involved a great deal of listening and there were not a few evenings when she came back home late after spending a few hours with someone in the church. J Nam concluded that everyone, even very quiet people, will talk if they realise that they'll really be listened to and not judged. After a trusting relationship had been formed, it was occasionally right to gently challenge a person's wrong thinking. Often that came through applying the Bible when they looked at it together.

As well as Alpha courses we occasionally put on extra activities for the believers to supplement the regular cycle of services and mid-week meetings. Sometimes we had a guest speaker or watched a dvd together usually followed by a time for discussion. We looked at a variety of different topics such as church health, spiritual warfare, bringing up teenagers, other religions and Christian funerals. We also ran what we called a 'Marriage Refresh Course' which ran for a few weeks on Sunday afternoons. It ended with a short service of recommitment at which our advisor pastor agreed to lead each couple was given a certificate which Angela had helped us to make. The course was perhaps of extra significance for those who had married Shinto style in their non-Christian days.

Another activity was for me to meet each church member one by one to ask them how their lives were, especially their relationship with God. I'd heard that the pastor at Atsubetsu was doing this and thought it sounded an excellent idea, although I wasn't sure if this was common practice among Japanese pastors.

We also had a variety of social events such as barbeques and picnics, visits to parks and tennis. Church folk even tried cricket (a minor sport in Japan) on one occasion. The husband of a missionary couple assigned to Tonden while they were at language school gave some basic lessons and everyone had a go. One other communal activity was the bi-annual 'big clean'; apparently this was a regular practice in Japanese churches, at least in our denomination. Church members worked together after the Sunday service to clean the whole building, and then we had lunch together as usual – usually Japanese curry and rice.

All the social activities contributed to building a family atmosphere and were also good for inviting non-Christians.

2009

As the new year began, we knew that we had only seven months left before our return to England. With discussions ongoing, the church members had soon to vote on whether to invite the associate pastor to be their pastor in April or not. They voted against calling him. We think it may have been somewhat of a shock for him, but no promise had been made at any point. Some members didn't understand why he wasn't invited but we and the church officers felt it was the right decision even though there was no other candidate on the horizon. Later he became the pastor of a church in another part of Hokkaido. Sadly, his wife never recovered from cancer and passed away about two years later.

That Easter there were another two baptisms. One was a teenager, a daughter of a church member and a good friend of Angela. The other was a young man from another part of Hokkaido, who had become engaged to a church member who'd been baptised a year earlier. He'd believed in Christ after studying with me and his journey to faith had been quite smooth. Soon afterwards they married and we had a wedding service in our church. It was a joyful occasion though it was a pity that none of his relatives (all non-Christian) came. They attended the reception which was held in a hotel several months later.

The time for us to leave was fast approaching. We had no definite plans to come back to Japan after Home Assignment and so instead of storing our belongings in the warehouse that OMF rented we shipped almost everything back to the UK. We sent them to what was to be our new home in Cambridge. It was an amazing provision from the Lord that the missionary couple at Tonden owned a house in Cambridge which they were happy for us to rent at a low rate.

Angela had to say goodbye to staff and friends at Hokkaido International School. Only a week or two before we left, she took part in a school "Noh' (traditional Japanese dance-drama) performance. She was quite excited about our move to Cambridge, especially as we'd heard that she had a place in her preferred sixth form college. But she was also somewhat apprehensive and sad to leave Japan, which had, in effect, become her homeland. The Home Assignments in England had never been regarded as time at home.

Looking back now we were not sufficiently aware of the challenges she would face living in England long term.

Our final Sunday arrived. The final service and my final sermon. A number of extra folks turned up; primarily those who attended mid-week events, such as the English class, but rarely – if ever – came on Sundays. There was a farewell gathering with lots of tasty food, short speeches, photos, and many goodbyes. We appreciated everyone's kindness but it was hard to take it all in as we were very tired from packing our things and clearing our flat. I found the actual day of departure more emotional. There were about 20 people who saw us off at Sapporo airport, including a few from Atsubetsu Church. A boy of about 10 gave me a lovely little note of appreciation he'd written which touched me when I read it during the short flight to Tokyo. We stayed for a few days at the OMF guest home and were able to see Ogo-san, my friend from my single days in Tokyo, 25 years earlier. Then we took the long-haul flight to Heathrow, London. Although we didn't know it our 14 years as OMF missionaries in Japan were over.

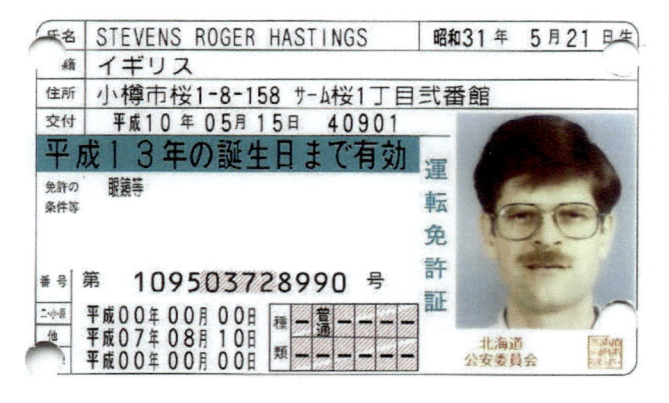

My Japanese driving licence

PART TWO
Ministry to Japanese in Cambridge (2009-22)

CAMBRIDGE is a unique and beautiful city - at least the old, central part of it! The house we were to live in was a small late-Victorian terraced house. It was in a convenient area only 20 minutes on foot from the city centre. Two or three days after arriving in England we set off for our new home.

We didn't really know anyone in Cambridge; there was an OMF couple with whom we had some recent email contact and another Christian couple who had hosted us for one night two years earlier. We found the house was almost bare, though there was a fridge and a washing machine. The things we'd shipped from Japan weren't due to arrive for another month though we had some of the stuff that had been in storage in the church hall in Watford. Thankfully someone from Rock Baptist Church, the church we were to attend, had set up camp-beds for us and another kind church person was fixing a dining room table and chairs for us when we arrived. We quickly bought a sofa at a local charity shop, started getting our new home set up, had a short holiday and began to explore our new surroundings.

A few things surprised us about life in the UK compared to Japan. On the one hand we were able to buy a mobile phone in a supermarket (in Japan there was a slow application process) but on the other hand setting up internet was much slower than in Japan and a special bed with a desk underneath ordered for Angela took five to six weeks to arrive.

We began attending Rock church and were able to join their weekend away, Angela then started at the Sixth Form College and our stuff from Japan arrived. God had provided all our needs and everything seemed to be fitting into place nicely.

Yet it wasn't home. There were no friends around, nor family, no role at a new church. And there were many indefinable little things. It *felt* strange that nobody glanced at me in the street and that most people were speaking English. We were out of touch with popular culture and even many worship songs at church were unknown to us.

Some things were fun but overall, all the changes meant we were facing reverse culture shock. This was harder for Angela and I than for J Nam; probably because of her personality and her having lower expectations as England wasn't her homeland. It helped being able to meet some Japanese at the Cambridge Japanese Christian Fellowship (JCF) and an OMF British–Japanese family but even then, it wasn't the same as being in Japan (should we speak Japanese or English?). Looking back now we are grateful for our supporters who continued in prayer for us. In fact, nobody stopped being prayer-partners as can happen when missionaries who return for home-side ministry are no longer regarded as 'real' missionaries.

Officially we were on Home Assignment, a time intended for rest and renewal, for reconnecting with family, friends and supporters and for reporting about our work at churches and to the OMF leadership. We were not supposed to begin for nine months or more our Japanese Diaspora Returnee Ministries (DRM) work. (JDRM since early 2024 has been renamed Japanese Returnee Focus). There was still the slight possibility of our going back to Japan after two years. In practice we didn't get much rest mainly because we soon began to meet more Japanese – though that was something we were actually quite keen on doing!

For me it was at 'The Barn', an international students coffee bar run by Friends International. For J Nam it was through helping out at a Japanese Mums and toddlers' group that the Japanese Christian Fellowship ran and attending an international women's group at a city centre church where around half the attendees were Japanese wives. As well as this I was occasionally asked to speak at London JCF Sunday afternoon worship and so met Japanese folk there.

It was interesting how we met a Japanese lady who was learning English as a Foreign Language at one of the many language schools. She had met a couple outside Ely Cathedral who were doing outreach handing out tea. She loved tea, they got talking and a Bible study had begun. However, studying in English was too difficult for her and so the couple decided to introduce her to Japanese speakers at our church in Cambridge. They took her to a Sunday service but unfortunately, we were at a different church that day. However, an alert church member took her details and through this we were able to meet up. She showed some interest in the Bible and started coming to our house. We had a meal, during which we chatted mostly in English and then had Bible study in Japanese. This set a pattern – though a few only wanted to speak in Japanese – which we followed with students, researchers and the occasional businessman for several years.

We were always curious to find out why someone had come to England rather than another English-speaking country (especially the USA, which is the most popular). The usual reasons were a particular interest in British culture and history or, in the case of business people and many researchers, because they had been sent to Britain. However, this lady's reason was different and one we'd never heard of before – nor since. After we'd got to know her quite well, she told us. It was because she had been a British person in a previous life. This had been 'revealed' to her when under a state of hypnosis and she had even said that when hypnotised she had lived in Cornwall – a place she had never heard of before.

We were very surprised and didn't quite know how to respond. What struck me most was the absolute conviction she had about reincarnation as against her attitude to Jesus and the Bible which she found interesting but not definitely true or relevant. When she went back to Japan, we managed to link her up with OMF missionaries and we kept in touch with her, including meeting her in Japan. As far as we know she has not yet put her faith in Jesus.

As well as having small numbers to our home for a meal and Bible study we also followed the practice of other OMF workers in arranging food parties for larger numbers. We made it clear that families were welcome. Once or twice, we hosted but because our house was very small, we more often held them in the homes of church folk who wanted to be involved. The hosts provided some food, occasionally Japanese Christian Fellowship folk brought contributions while most food (Korean as well as Japanese) was prepared by J Nam. We decided against having any Bible talk but gave a word of welcome in which we mentioned that we and the hosts were Christians. We also said that churches were usually good places to meet people – and places to find out about Christianity – and emphasised that non-Christians are also welcome to attend. Japanese usually think that church is only for Christians. One person who started coming to food parties and our house was someone who was doing post-doc research, the first of quite a number of 'high-powered' researchers – mostly in scientific and medical matters – that we met during our years in Cambridge. Although highly educated, almost all had extremely little knowledge of the Bible.

Christmas day with Japanese students at our house in Cambridge

As in Japan Christmas was a great time for meeting lots of people and sharing the Good News of Christ. In co-operation with Cambridge JCF, we hired a church and had a carol service followed by food, the food always drew people! The event attracted around 50 or more Japanese, including children, every year. I usually gave the main message in English with someone – usually Angela – translating. We often had a short quiz about Christmas which was popular and helped engender a relaxed atmosphere before the children went out for their own programme. We also gave everyone some literature in Japanese and information about our churches' Christmas services. When possible, we had a Japanese Christian give their testimony. It was difficult to assess the impact of Christmas outreach but a few people started coming to regular events and new contacts were made. The Easter season was also an opportunity to speak about Christ but, not surprisingly, numbers at our meetings then were distinctly lower.

2010

Angela studied hard at Sixth Form College, but struggled to make friends both there and at the church youth group. For her it was culture shock rather than reverse-culture shock but beyond this she was also dealing with the issues that most TCKs face. TCK stands for 'Third Culture Kid'; the three cultures refer to the culture of their parents, the culture of the country they have lived in for a significant number of years and the cultural ties they share in common with all TCKs. In Angela's case, it was more complex as J Nam is Korean and also has some German influence. The apparently simple question when meeting someone, 'Where are you from?' was not easy for her to answer! The fact that almost all the young people she came into contact with, both at school and church, were white British intensified the feeling of being out of place. In these circumstances we were thankful for our close family atmosphere and for Angela's definite Christian faith, both which gave her much needed support. Although there are positives in being a TCK, such as gaining a broader outlook on life, the years at sixth form and then at university were tough for Angela and it didn't get that much easier in the years immediately after. Even now the awareness of being a TCK remains but she has a much stronger sense of her primary identity as based on being a child of God rather than on her nationality or anything else.

Whenever Angela met Japanese people, she invariably enjoyed it. This happened mainly through our contacts in Cambridge and she was happy to get involved with JDRM events, especially the Christmas Carol Service and Food Party. She regularly had important roles to play such as interpreting Bible messages, helping with children's programmes and preparing power point presentations. She also got involved with the youth programme at an annual conference for Japanese churches in Europe. Starting in Spain in August 2010 we attended this conference for a number of years. It was good to gather for fellowship with large numbers of Japanese Christians though the style of worship was often rather formal for us. After attending these conferences, the three of us enjoyed staying on in the country for a few days holiday.

In mid-December 2010 there was a great shock when the German husband of one of the Cambridge JCF ladies collapsed during a church carol service and died soon after. She was still in her 30's, had three children and was pregnant. It was a devastating experience for her and her children. Thankfully she had a very supportive church. We and Cambridge JCF also did what we could to help at such a critical time. Eventually she was to leave Cambridge and move to Germany.

2011

As we continued to look for ways to meet Japanese I volunteered once a month at the Round Church visitor centre where I occasionally met Japanese, mainly tourists, as well as people from many other countries around the world. Another activity we arranged was having outings to London for families, visiting the British Museum and the British Library, where we pointed out exhibits that have connections with the Bible. Also, in London we once visited the Florence Nightingale Museum. Nightingale is well known in Japan, especially in medical circles; but that she was strongly influenced by the Bible appears to be unknown. In Cambridge we conducted our own guided walks where we could naturally show people buildings that mark Christian influence, both in history and today.

Outside the Florence Nightingale Museum in London

However, we particularly wanted to meet more men and I wondered if I could start a men's social group of some kind? A sports group such as football or golf would likely be popular, but the drawback was that I was not into sport! In the end the idea came to do something I knew was done in Japan and start a dinner club.

The plan was simple. I chose a restaurant and emailed men inviting them to come along to enjoy food and socialising together. And that was basically it. They were asked to give a definite reply because I needed to book a table. Almost all my contacts were the husbands of ladies J Nam had met at the Mums and toddlers' group or the International Women's group. I also invited men from our church and other local churches who were interested in meeting Japanese. When we met at the chosen restaurant I tried to arrange it so that the native English speakers were evenly spaced among the Japanese. There were usually around six Japanese and two to three others. After the meal there was the option to spend further time together, usually in a pub. Most usually came along.

Later we had special Easter meetings, reserving a room at a pub which gave more privacy and meant we could have activities after the meal such as a quiz and a talk about the meaning of Easter.

This "Men's Meal Group" (I never came up with a catchier name) continued for almost nine years until it was finally killed off by the Covid pandemic. Many men were contacted and had a taste (hopefully positive!) of what Christians were like – very likely this was the first time for them to ever meet Christians.

The first Men's Meal meeting on March 13th 2011 is etched in my mind because we met only a day after the huge East Japan earthquake, tsunami and nuclear disaster in Fukushima. Naturally we all talked about it but although it was known that things were very bad, events were still unfolding and they were to get even worse. As they did, I felt shock and pain for the people of Japan and was particularly concerned for those we knew there. Added to this we were in the midst of planning a ministry visit to Japan that summer. For a while we thought we might have to cancel it but eventually decided to go ahead as our schedule did not include any of the devastated areas. When in the Tokyo area we noticed that there were some shortages of electricity; less lighting on buildings, some restrictions on the use of air-conditioners and escalators not running at some stations. However, this didn't stop us getting together with some of the folk we'd met in Cambridge and visiting Sapporo. We also visited Korea.

That August Angela was delighted to be offered a place at Cambridge University. She entered Homerton College which happened to be almost next-door to her Sixth Form College. She got involved with CICCU and for one year was the international rep for her college. We thought she would meet some Japanese students, but to our surprise there were hardly any at the university during her three years there.

2012

A regular Mums and toddlers' group was a part of our Cambridge ministry. As J Nam got to know better the young mothers from the mums and toddlers' group she started a Bible discussion group in our

Mums and toddlers' group was a regular part of our Cambridge ministry

home. A few came – how much to chat and how much to look at the Bible wasn't clear. However, there was one who was definitely keen to study and we asked our prayer partners to pray for her a number of times. She had been brought up as a Roman Catholic (her cousin was a priest) and knew that Jesus had died for all people, including her, but she didn't know how to respond. In Japan she had watched the film '*Passion*', depicting the crucifixion, with tears streaming down her face but that impression had gradually faded. After about a year of studying, including occasional meetings one-on-one, J Nam led her to put her faith in Jesus. We prayed for her husband but saw no response; I never even met him. From what J Nam heard he was a classic example of a workaholic

Throughout our time in Cambridge, we put a high priority on

networking with anyone reaching out to internationals. I regularly dropped into the cafes run by Friends International (FI) with the primary aim of meeting Japanese, which they accepted. Early on, at 'The Barn' cafe, I had met Kotoe, a friendly, outgoing young lady in her early 30's who was at one of the many English language schools in Cambridge. We found out that she was in a FI Bible study but her English was not at a high enough level to get much out of it. She admitted to us that she was thinking of stopping and so we invited her to our house for Bible study in Japanese, while encouraging her to continue studying in English. We learned that she was home-staying with a Christian couple and going with them to their church so was having quite a lot of exposure to the Gospel. She made good progress in her understanding, but had not quite come through to faith by the time she had to return to Japan. However, a few months later she came back – staying with the same home-stay family again – and after some weeks put her faith in Jesus. We began to disciple and prepare her for going back to Japan and living as a Christian there. To help her find and settle in a church we wrote a letter about her journey of faith for her to show to the pastor of any church she hoped to join. A few weeks before leaving the UK, in August 2013, Kotoe was baptised at her church and I had the privilege of assisting one of the church staff in the ceremony. I asked – and she answered – the pre-baptismal questions in both English and Japanese.

We kept in contact by Skype to encourage her in her new faith, especially as she didn't know any Christians or churches in Japan. Helping returnees like her to find a suitable, evangelical church is extremely important but not always simple. There are many different denominations and independent churches in Japan as well as "Christian' cults and some modern Buddhist groups that call their buildings 'churches'. We checked the internet ourselves but usually asked a lady with OMF in Japan who, with her husband, had a lot of experience working with overseas Japanese and returnees. They were giving training at churches all over Japan to make them more effective in welcoming and nurturing returnees. They were also instrumental in setting up regional returnee groups in Japan.

Eventually Kotoe found a church where she felt at home through a returnee group, we told her about. When we visited Japan two years later, we were happy to attend the Sunday morning service with her. The pastor and his wife – also a pastor and who had taken her through some Bible studies – greeted us warmly. A few years later she married a committed Christian and they visited Cambridge for part of their honeymoon.

In August 2012 we began a six-month Home Assignment (HA), later extended to nine months. As we were in the UK and our 'Home' was our house in Cambridge this didn't change things much for us. We couldn't stop meeting with our non-Christian contacts and because of the need to visit supporters and participate at OMF conferences our lives were as busy as ever, if not more so. This issue was recognised by the Diaspora Returnee Ministries leadership and eventually a new system was put in place.

In the autumn an opportunity to start a new Bible study occurred. A Japanese businessman to whom I was teaching English told me that his working hours were shorter than when he was in Japan. Having more spare time one of the things he wanted to do was, "to learn about Christianity." I couldn't do that for him during the English lessons as his company was paying for them but I lent him a Japanese New Testament. That didn't seem enough for him so I suggested having Japanese Bible study after our English class. As his wife also showed some interest J Nam came along and all four of us studied together in their home. After they went back to Japan, we studied by Skype though his wife stopped and the two of us met less often than before. However, we have continued even until the time of writing. I have sometimes wondered if it's worth carrying on for so long. J Nam and I have sometimes had the same question regarding other contacts, but our conclusion is that as long as a person shows a willingness to go on studying the Bible we will continue with them. We try to encourage them to go to church and/or contact local believers, send them useful links and wait in hope that God, by His Spirit, will reveal Jesus to the person's heart.

2013

A new experience this year was the publication of, *"Buddhist Priest meets Jesus"* that I'd translated from Japanese. Although it was only half a book the whole process took several years. It began when I came across the book in a Christian book store in Sapporo when we were at Tonden Church. As it looked interesting, I decided to try reading it for the ongoing language study project we were expected to do. It was a fascinating testimony of how a Japanese Buddhist priest, who was looking for the purpose of life in Buddhism, found the answer through faith in Christ when he was doing post-graduate studies in South Korea. As the story was so interesting and inspiring it occurred to me that it would be great if it could be made available in English. So, I decided to have a go! Little-by-little the translation proceeded and when it was finally completed after we'd returned to Britain, I found a publisher. It's still available and a great read, especially for anyone with an interest in God's work among Japanese people, other East Asians or Buddhists. Copies can be obtained from Loxwood Press.

2014

The year started with a funeral when Eric, one of my best friends, died from cancer on January 4th. It was not a surprise except it happened earlier than expected. I had met him in 1985 and, though our backgrounds in some ways were very different, we got on really well together. Eric was a great encourager, showed a genuine interest in our ministry and family and was a man of prayer, especially as illness increasingly restricted him in his last few years. He could also see the funny side to life and the two of us often enjoyed having a good laugh together. Chatting on the phone a few weeks before he died, he spoke confidently of the hope he had in Christ; "I'm looking forward to meeting the Lord" were virtually the last words I heard Eric say.

As our ministry in Cambridge continued God opened doors to Japanese further afield. A prayer partner couple introduced us to two Japanese Christian ladies from their church in St Albans. One of them in particular was eager to reach out to her non-Christian Japanese friends and asked if we could assist her? The result was a monthly

Bible study in her home, though our first meeting was in the home of another lady at which J Nam taught a Korean cooking class and gave a short testimony. I became the leader of this ladies' study, largely because I needed to drive J Nam (public transport wasn't convenient) to St Albans. The group continues to meet though some have left and others have joined and there are now more Christians. As a result of the coronavirus pandemic we started meeting online and this has become the norm since we moved away from Cambridge. Nearly all of the participants are permanent residents in the UK and most of them have lived away from Japan for many years. It may well be because of this that they are more open and ready to share during our discussion times.

Another opportunity opened up in Norwich. A Scottish lady had a monthly English Bible study in her home for Japanese students on Sunday afternoons. This was followed by supper together. Most of the members were post-graduate students studying Overseas Development. We started making the occasional visit and led the study in Japanese. One of the groups believed in Jesus at church and became very definite and committed.

When it was time for her to return to Japan a couple of years later, she decided she would tell her non-Christian parents that she'd become a Christian as soon as possible – that meant at the airport when they met her. We felt that might perhaps be a little too soon and advised her to seek God's timing about when and how to tell her parents. We didn't want to dampen her zeal, but on the other hand felt that it might not be wise to bluntly tell them at the airport. New believers are usually nervous and hesitant about when and what to say to their parents and friends but in her case our concern was the opposite. As it turned out she did tell her parents at the airport, they were strongly opposed to her decision and became angry as she tried to explain the Gospel. Things became very difficult for her as she wasn't allowed to go to church or even hum Christian songs. For a while we met with her online, especially when she had no other fellowship. Things improved when she moved out of her parents' home about a year later, moved to Tokyo and was free to go to church.

Later we were pleased to hear that she had got baptised and was continuing in the Christian life.

That September we joined a group from our church and a few other believers who were starting a church plant in a suburb of Cambridge. After a while they decided to support us financially on a regular basis (the previous church had helped with some of our expenses) which was a great help as until then our support levels were often only just sufficient to continue as members of OMF. They also regularly prayed for us and asked for updates on our work.

That autumn we did a lot of travelling. Angela couldn't come as she had just started at the OMF UK national office as an intern. We attended the DRM International conference in Colorado, USA, going via Iceland and staying there two nights for a belated celebration of our silver wedding anniversary. Seeing boiling mud and water and a geyser regularly spouting was the main highlight. Then on to the US.

The conference site, Glen Eyrie, international HQ of the Navigators, is in a beautiful area with some spectacular rock formations. It was an excellent time of great teaching and good fellowship, including reunion with a few OMFers we'd known in Japan. Furthermore, I received a fresh reassurance that being in JDRM in Cambridge was God's place for me – at least for the time being.

After getting back to the UK it was less than a week before we set off for Japan. It was a good time seeing returnees from Cambridge and folk from churches in Sapporo. As usual we also visited Korea where we visited the cemetery in Seoul where the remains of one of J Nam's brothers were interred. He had sadly died of cancer the previous year, but it was a comfort to know that he had believed in Christ some years before. A week later a large number gathered one evening in the old family home, which was in a very rural area in the far south. This was for a memorial ceremony for J Nam's mother who had died a year earlier at the age of 95. For the last few months of her life, she had lived in a Christian care home. The ceremony was led by one of J Nam's brothers-in-law as he was the oldest male among the relations. He conducted it according to the traditional Confucian way but when he finished, he generously asked if any of the Christians present would like to take over and perform a Christian ceremony. J Nam and one of her sisters prayed. The next day we all visited the newly-made family grave which meant a short walk up into the hills. On the tomb stone it was good to see a Bible verse. As well as this I was very surprised to see my name in the names listed there. Apparently, as I'd married into J Nam's family, this was normal practice in Korean culture.

When we got back to the UK, we were very tired but there was little time to rest because of our part in preparing and leading the regular JCF Christmas service. In retrospect we think we should have made the Japan trip a few months later!

J Nam and I with Kotoe outside her church in Nagoya

2015

As I continued to attend a Friends International (FI) cafe for students I became more aware of the age gap. Approaching the age of 60 it occurred to me that I could be a grandfather of the younger students! However, with the Japanese and other East Asians this didn't seem to matter much. At a special FI event we were introduced to a student at a language school who showed a keen interest in the Bible, and through him met three more young men. It wasn't long before he accepted our invitation and, with one or two others, started coming to our house for food and Japanese Bible study. However, out of the blue his sister, who was only in her 20's, died from a heart attack. We hardly knew what to say or do. What can you say in such tragic circumstances? He went back to Japan. We wondered if we would ever see him or hear from him again. Sadly, we never did.

Near the end of this year our church, Christ Church. Trumpington, started an international cafe. We were fully involved from its early days and for several years we were to be on the leadership team. I enjoyed greeting people at the reception, chatting with visitors and giving occasional presentations which were usually about something from Christian history, such as Martin Luther, C. S. Lewis, Alfred the Great and the Pilgrim Fathers. J Nam was involved in some of the cooking sessions, gave a talk about her life and faith and invited quite a few of her contacts – almost all were Japanese ladies.

2016

At the start of 2016 I was coming to the end of a Home Assignment and again facing challenges in the area of financial support. Without 80% of my budget coming through regular donations I wouldn't be able to return to the 'field' as a full OMF member unless I found additional sources of funding, such as more English teaching. It was quite a stressful time but enough was provided just in time! This was mainly through an extremely large gift from a prayer partner and so I was able to start a new term as a DRM worker. Truly God moved a mountain. Again, I felt that God had confirmed I was in the right place and doing the right work.

Not long after this a married lady was baptised just before she returned to Japan. We had got to know her and her family quite well in the five years they'd spent in Cambridge, though in the process of coming to faith Christians of other churches had the major role. Her husband didn't oppose her decision and came to the baptism and took photographs. He had also attended a course for international seekers, but when he was back in Japan his interest apparently disappeared.

Two years later, when we visited Japan, she invited us to their home in Kyoto. We had a brief opportunity to give her some encouragement before her husband arrived home from work. As usual with returnees she wasn't finding it easy to adapt to life as a Christian in Japan and unfortunately this was compounded by divisions in the church she was attending. Some time after this the husband's job took him back to Cambridge for a few years. She joined him for most of the time, linking up with her previous church again and continues to pray for him to come to faith. When she went back to Japan this time she adapted better to life as a Christian there. This was helped by her church situation becoming stable.

Gate/entrance to a Shinto shrine

2017

As the monthly "Men's Meal" meetings continued they led to more interaction with men in other ways. With a few I started language exchange meetings. We'd meet – usually in a cafe – and spend half the time using English and the other half Japanese. Sometimes it was just free conversation, other times there would be some teaching. I found it helpful to suggest a topic, perhaps a short article to read together followed by conversation based on it. Through these meetings we'd get to know each other better and in one or two cases it later became a bilingual Bible study. A few men showed a definite interest in Christianity and the Bible from early on. Two joined me in a bilingual Bible study and we decided to meet in a pub, which was usually quiet enough. Once or twice, I invited them to our house. One of them had already read through the entire Bible – extremely unusual for a non-Christian. The other one was so keen that he made his own notes as we studied and sometimes printed articles from the internet and brought them to our meetings to show us. After a while I discovered that his aunt was a Christian. When the two men returned to Japan in 2018, we set up separate meetings using Skype to continue studying. However, just as I was beginning to look for a church to recommend to the latter, he suddenly said he was really tired and asked for 'a break of several months. I must admit I was surprised and disappointed by this. Thinking about it now he may well have been going through reverse culture-shock. Whatever the case the 'several months' lengthened to several years, though we've had occasional contact through Facebook.

Another man, coming to the Men's Meal for the first time, asked me whether he could come to my church. Consequently, he came about three times a month and eventually attended a "Christianity Explored 'course. The church presented him with a bilingual New Testament on his last Sunday. Before he returned to Japan, he and I started seeker's Bible study in Japanese and this continued online thereafter

At our usual Christmas carol service and food event that year around 100 people attended. It was probably our highest number ever and more than half were non-Christians.

2018

The year 2018 turned out to be greatly significant. In January we booked flights for a week in Korea and three weeks in Japan in April-May. Angela, who was now working as a para-legal, was to be with us for two weeks. As on previous occasions our goal was to meet up with returnees and see folk from the two churches we had led. First, however, we spent a few days in Korea where, as usual, we met various relatives. In Seoul we were taken by some of J Nam's sisters to a high-class restaurant for a buffet lunch to celebrate J Nam's seventieth birthday – according to the old Korean system which counts your age as one when you are born. So, by the Western way of counting, she was only 69 years old!

Then on to Japan where we had several memorable occasions. In Sapporo we wanted to visit Tonden Church. Following Japanese etiquette, we had emailed the part-time pastor a few weeks earlier to ask if it was all right to attend a Sunday service. Not only was he happy about that he also asked me if I would preach at the service. I could hardly refuse and, encouragingly, found that after nearly nine years away from living in Japan my language ability was still adequate.

In Kansai when staying near Kobe I had an unpleasant encounter with a giant centipede three to four inches long in the bathroom. Fortunately, I wasn't stung by it and managed to kill it with the handle of a broom or something. At Osaka International Church, where a few returnees joined us, I happened to meet a lady who had attended the Friends International, 'The Barn' cafe in Cambridge nearly 20 years earlier. Some years later she had become a Christian in Switzerland. The seed sown had borne fruit. In Kyoto we met up with two returnee students from Cambridge and took them to a Bible study and meal hosted by a Japanese lady.

In Tokyo we visited a church at which two university students we knew attended. Mana and Seichiro were sister and brother and we had known them since they were very small in Sapporo – their parents had been baptised in 2007. After the service, when people were mingling over coffee, I overheard a few lines of Seichiro's conversation with a friend about us. A friend asked them, "Who are these two geezers (probably thinking I didn't understand Japanese)?" The brother replied, "Oh, they first told us about Jesus when we were little kids." I must admit that I was touched by this. Seeds that had been sown by us and others more than 15 years before had borne fruit. He went on to be baptised a few months later. His sister had already been baptised.

My first-ever Japanese friend, Sumi, from university days 40 years earlier, came to this same church service with his wife. They'd come from Kagoshima, over 800 miles away, though they also visited one of their sons who lived in Tokyo. We all had lunch together and as we chatted, we were surprised but pleased to hear that his daughter was a Christian, working in Cambodia. Some days later I met my best friend from my Tokyo days (1982-85), Ogo-san, in a restaurant. Our time together was not unusual but it turned out to be the last time we would meet. Some months later he died from a massive heart attack. Though I was aware he had some health issues I was really shocked and saddened, though comforted by remembering his faith in Christ.

The final event of our three weeks in Japan was to attend the 'Global Returnee Conference' at which over 300 returnees gathered. They had believed in Jesus in various countries all over the world, though most came to faith in the U.S.A. A few people we knew personally were there. It was a vivid picture of the potential of reaching Japanese while they are overseas. The conference was held in a hotel that was only a few minutes' walk away from a breathtaking view of the magnificent snow-capped Mount Fuji.

Mount Fuji

The whole trip to Japan was really worthwhile but it was also hectic, right to the end. When we were heading back to Tokyo after the returnee conference the coach got stuck in a massive traffic jam and was about three hours late in arriving. By the time we'd found our hotel late in the evening we only had time for about four or five hours sleep before leaving for Haneda Airport to catch our plane to London Heathrow. Once back home it wasn't long before we resumed our activities with Japanese, got back into the rhythm of church life and, being on Home Assignment, started visiting supporters. In the summer, with Angela, we took the train to Edinburgh which was the location for the Japanese Churches in Europe annual conference. As usual we added on a few days holiday.

For the next few months, it was ministry as normal. Then at our usual bilingual Christmas carol service we had good numbers with the majority being non-Christians. Guest speaker Chris Pain gave a challenge to be like the wise men who made the long journey to find and worship the newborn, King. A week or so later it was Christmas Day but we had decided against our usual practice of inviting Japanese to our house. Somehow, we all seemed to be more tired than usual. I remember on one day a few weeks earlier I felt unusually weary after cycling home from a language exchange session. Despite this none of us had the slightest inkling of what was about to happen.

At about 2am on Christmas Day I had to make a night-time visit to the loo. I had an uncomfortable sensation like indigestion in my abdomen but soon fell asleep again thinking it would be gone in the morning. However, I woke up still feeling the same and stayed in bed all morning. Medicine didn't help, I felt a bit nauseous and couldn't face any food. What was the matter with me? Bored by staying in bed I managed to get downstairs and lay on the sofa. Finally, I asked Angela to check the NHS website which she did and then she phoned them. After a few questions to her, me and my wife they said an ambulance would be on its way. Somewhat surprisingly it arrived quickly and after a few tests we heard the totally unexpected words, "I'm sorry to say you're having a heart attack."

I was taken to the ambulance and within a few minutes we were speeding off to hospital, J Nam with me. As it was Christmas Day there was no traffic and upon arrival I was taken straight into the operating theatre. Someone said the operation would have a 94% (or thereabouts) chance of success – did I want to go ahead? What could I say? "I'm in your hands", I answered, but was aware that ultimately, I was in God's hands and that gave me peace, though at times I felt close to tears. I knew that the Lord was with me, and that gave me real hope even if I were to die. A consultant, who called me 'squire', operated and inserted a stent. After that, I stayed in hospital until New Year's Eve. It was the Royal Papworth, the UK's leading heart and lung hospital – Prince Philip had been treated there some years previously. I was so thankful for the staff and for the many acts of kindness from family and friends from church. Above all, I was and still am thankful to God for His loving and saving hand on my life.

A turning point
2019-2022

DECEMBER 25 2018 was a turning point in our lives and to some extent in our ministry among Japanese people. The year 2019 was to be very much about health matters. Recovery from a heart attack takes time, though in some respects perhaps not as long as one might think. Following medical guidance, I started doing gentle exercise as soon as possible and joined a rehab group in February. However, I was also twice dispatched to A&E by my GP when I wasn't feeling too good. On one of these visits, I was told that my heart had been permanently damaged, very likely because I hadn't known for several hours that I was having a heart attack. There were some other medical issues that emerged in 2019; an infected foot (so bad that I was asked if I minded having a photo taken of it –perhaps for the NHS website!), an extremely sensitive tooth and being diagnosed with diabetes type 2. We were very thankful that within a few months it was found that my diabetes was in remission.

Despite these health issues, I gradually got back into ministry activities, though with a reduced work schedule. The Men's Meal numbers began to fall and later in the year drastically so. Eventually it fizzled out almost completely and I felt it was time to close it down

– even before the Covid pandemic. It had been running for more than eight years and I had met a lot of Japanese men through it.

I was also able to join some OMF events and that summer, following generally positive advice from a cardiac consultant, I flew with J Nam to Germany for the DRM team conference, followed by a short holiday in France. I was now feeling almost normal despite the heat which went over 40C on one day!

As the year 2020 began who could have forecasted Coronavirus and the enormous impact it was to have on the world? From the first lock-down announcement in March all of our ministry, indeed virtually everything in our lives – as for so many people – went online.

It took a while to get used to some of the technical issues but fortunately Angela was around to give us help. She also prepared power point activities for the Mum' and toddlers' group as it met online. She had been planning to go to Korea after quitting her job as a para-legal on January 31st but the pandemic prevented that. That summer she took an intensive online course in TESOL (Teaching English to Speakers of Other Languages) and gradually gained individual students online.

My Bible studies with returnees by Skype continued. Otherwise, I had more time to focus on reading and on writing projects. Meanwhile J Nam's Bible study with two seekers became a weekly event because they all had more spare time. One day, one lady's computer suddenly stopped working and because of this J Nam had the opportunity to explain the Gospel in some detail to the other lady and led her in a prayer of faith. The weekly study continued, but now there were natural opportunities for the new believer to speak about what had happened to her. As well as this online study J Nam's Bible studies and prayer meetings with JCF (Japanese Christian Fellowship) ladies all went online.

Our attention began to be directed towards another matter. Our landlord and his family had arrived back in the UK at the end of March and that meant we had to move out of his house as had been agreed from the beginning of our tenancy. He was extremely kind and put no pressure on us by setting a deadline. Moreover, the Covid pandemic meant it was going to be a while before moving was possible and so we had time to investigate the different options, hoping to stay in Cambridge, or at least nearby. However, it soon became clear that to rent would be far too expensive; we realised even more how generous our landlord was in the rate he was charging us.

We applied for council housing and looked into the Shared ownership scheme, but neither proved to be suitable. So, we started looking further afield to find somewhere affordable and as our search continued into 2021 J Nam's attention was one day drawn to a place we'd never considered. It's amusing to recall my initial reaction; "Why on earth would I want to live in Peterborough?" To cut a long story short we were able to buy a flat. We had never imagined buying a property of our own would ever be possible. It was in a good location on the outskirts and we moved in on October 7th 2021. Though our decision was driven very much by financial considerations, we felt that this was God's place for us. It's convenient for all our needs and yet less than a 10-minute walk to the countryside.

One matter of some concern was whether Peterborough was too far away for us to continue our Japanese ministry in Cambridge. But with the pandemic still around, all our regular activities were continuing online. Also going to Cambridge was less than an hour by car and it was only seven-and-a-half months to my retirement from OMF and the last four months of this were due to be a final Home Assignment when direct ministry would not be expected. The final consideration was that we had to move somewhere!

For Christmas 2021, as for the previous year, we arranged a carol service online. Numbers were low but a scientific researcher joined us. He was new to Christianity but very interested and already active in a large church in Cambridge. Soon after we started regular online meetings in Japanese at which he asked us a lot of questions. We were delighted when, a few weeks later, he put his faith in Jesus. Until he went back to Japan in July our meetings continued, including a visit from him. We did what we could to help prepare him for life in Japan as a Christian. His main challenge and concern were how to respond to his 'atheistic' wife who was worried about him becoming 'religious'. Back in Japan he found a small church near his house and for a while she reluctantly allowed him to go. We had some Zoom calls with him but that stopped and as we remember him in prayer now, we hope we can resume contact one day.

Our direct, 'coal-face' JDRM activity became somewhat less, though our regular online meetings all continued. Moreover my 'behind the scenes' ministry increased. I made a presentation at a half-day online conference, 'Japan on your Doorstep' sponsored by OMF and Japan Christian Link. It was about how history has impacted the 'flavour' of Japanese churches today. To my great surprise it turned out to be very popular – later I thought it was probably the link with the present in the title that had attracted people. In 2022 I made another presentation for the same online conference. I've also had a major role in the revision and updating of a small OMF book, "*A Christian Pocket Guide to the Japanese*". (It's due for publication in January 2025, under a new title, "*Sharing your Faith with your Japanese Neighbour.*" and is especially intended to assist Christians to reach out to Japanese who are overseas.)

In the last few months before my final Home Assignment there were very few meetings with supporters, partly owing to the ongoing covid pandemic. We also had a few unexpected hospital visits. J Nam went to A&E because of chest pains and about a week later in January 2022 I spent two nights in hospital with a concern about my heart condition. However online ministry continued for us both; I even began a new online study with one returnee using a book by a Japanese Christian author, Ayako Miura.

There were two events to wrap things up before retirement; my last OMF ministry review and a final Home Assignment Workshop. As it happened, I didn't attend the workshop until a few months after I'd retired. Then the day arrived that you never quite expect. On May 21 2022, my 66th birthday, I officially retired and became an Old Age Pensioner. I was no longer a full member of OMF International but became a co-worker since 2024 termed a volunteer as J Nam already was.

Postscript 2022-24
Life continues in retirement! Health concerns have not disappeared and I have to live with the condition of heart failure. We have become members of a large, lively, local church and are involved in various ways while at the same time our Japanese ministry – mostly online – continues. I've been working on this book and hope to do some more writing. A recent and big change has been Angela's marriage to Matthew and joining his church.

But what is retirement exactly? I feel I'm still coming to terms with what it means and involves. Is it, 'one long holiday', as a neighbour in Cambridge said? Or is it true that for the Christian there's no retirement? I think the answer depends on how we view the Christian life. If it's seen as 'working' for the Lord then, sooner or later, retirement in some form or another is no doubt inevitable. But if the Christian life is 'walking' with the Lord then clearly, we never retire from that.

"Regard the retirement years as a divinely-given opportunity for new adventure and achievement." wrote J Oswald Sanders. What new adventures and challenges might lie ahead for us? We cannot say we have no uncertainties about the future but we can say we believe that the Lord has good plans for the next stage of our lives, however long or short it may be. When we were married in 1989, as Psalm 48:14 had been given to us, we had the reference inscribed inside our wedding rings. We trust that we will never forget its words, "this is God, our God forever and ever. He will be our guide for ever."